Edie Melson and Rhonda Rhea combine laugh out loud humor with powerful biblical truth in *Unruffled*. If you long for peace in the middle of the chaos of life, don't miss this book!
~ Carol Kent, Speaker & Author, *He Holds My Hand: Experiencing God's Presence & Protection* (Tyndale)

I don't know too many women in ministry as busy as Rhonda and Edie. They keep more plates in the air than a professional juggler! So who better to lead us in not only surviving the chaos but thriving in it? With humor and grace, they bring profound Scriptural truth and guidance to anyone trying to keep their head above the water. Such a great read! You will finish encouraged and filled with hope. This one will definitely stay on my bedside shelf!
~ Julie Zine Coleman, *Unexpected Love: God's Heart Revealed through Jesus' Conversations with Women* (Thomas Nelson), Managing Editor at AriseDaily.com

The best two examples ever of how to *thrive in chaos* are Edie Melson and Rhonda Rhea. Yep—lotsa practice. These *Unruffled* gals truly know and live their stuff—effective and doable biblical how-tos in navigating the crazy lane of life without feeling totaled. I adore these ladies. You will, too!
~ Debora M. Coty, speaker and bestselling author of over 40 inspirational books, including the bestselling *Too Blessed to be Stressed* series, over one million books sold

Life is *so* hurried and hectic! Sometimes, despite our good intentions to regroup, readjust and reprioritize, God asks us to walk calm, confident and courageous *through* the confusion and chaos. When life feels stressful and imperfect, Edie and Rhonda help us *thrive* and live *Unruffled!*
~Pam Farrel, bestselling author of 49 books including *Discovering Joy in Philippians,* and *Men Are Like Waffles, Women Are Like Spaghetti*

If your to-do list is too long, chaos is your middle name, and the winds of change are whipping up in your life, this book is for you! With a gentle touch, calming truth, and a splash of humor here and there, *Unruffled* teaches you how to thrive when circumstances feel out of control. This dynamic duo holds out hands of hope full of biblical truth, providing the stability you need to make it through. Do yourself some good and grab hold of this book!

~Erica Wiggenhorn, Bible teacher and author of *Unexplainable Jesus: Rediscovering the God You Thought You Knew*

unRuffled

unRuffled

Thriving in Chaos

Edie Melson and Rhonda Rhea

Bold Vision Books
PO Box 2011
Friendswood, Texas 77549

Dedication

To our co-laborer, teacher, and friend,

Linda Evans Shepherd.

Your investment in our lives and ministries is a blessing that altogether amazes and beautifully unruffles.

Table of Contents

Part Five: Living Unruffled

Foreword

Karen Porter

Birds are dressed in feathers. Some are colorful and exotic; others are brown and easily camouflaged in the trees. When a bird's feathers are silky smooth, we are stunned at their beauty, but when the bird's feathers are ruffled, we can be sure all is not well.

The bird may be dusty and simply need a good bird bath. In the winter a bird may ruffle up its feathers to move air beneath his feathers so his skin will warm up the air and help him survive the cold temperatures. Some birds fluff out their feathers when frightened. And ruffled feathers could be a sign of sickness. Probably more than you wanted to know about feathers.

We ruffle our feathers too. When I feel dirty and grimy, I need a good cleansing from my mistakes and failures. Sometimes my ruffled feathers might be a cry for love or companionship or a kind word. When fear overwhelms, I ruffle my feathers to look tough and strong and menacing. Or my ruffled feathers might be a sign that I'm not feeling well emotionally or physically.

When Rhonda and Edie told me about this book, I thought it might be another book about how to get past trouble or problem. You know—one of those pull-yourself-up-by-the-boot-straps kind of books that says I don't have to live in chaos if I'll just take all the right steps toward healing and happiness.

But these two girls surprised me. This book isn't about getting through the storm or trouble. This book is about living in the middle of it. And by living, I mean living fully abundantly and happily in the eye of the chaotic hurricane named difficulty.

Now there's a concept I need to read about.

Not how I can push my way through or how I can get to the other side of trouble. Oh, I want to move forward for sure, but rescue, relief, and resolution can take a long time. How will I trust God when my feathers are still ruffled up? How will I cling to Him when I am shaking with the cold hand of rejection or depression on my shoulder? How will I face enemies when I am filled with fear? What do I do when the diagnosis is scary?

You and I need this message.

Don't wait for the calm or the solution or the answer—learn to thrive in the chaos and live Unruffled.

Karen Porter
Author of *If You Give A Girl A Giant*

Part One:

What Ruffles Your Feathers?

Why feathers? It's not just because we needed something to ruffle. We love the visual of a bird with beautiful, smooth feathers. They're able to fly, supported by this amazing combination of filament, muscle, and bone. Few wonders of nature are more beautiful than a delicate feather, yet they are incredibly resilient.

That said, there are also numerous references to feathers and wings throughout God's Word. The word pictures describing the love, protection, and provision of our heavenly Father are rich with application for us today.

A bird's feathers serve many purposes—from the tiny down feathers in the breast of a robin, to the strong pinions that allow an eagle to fly high above the earth. But can a bird's feathers get ruffled, or is that just an old saying that's crept into our vernacular today?

Birds sometimes ruffle their own feathers to clean them or to trap heat and help them stay warm. A bird's feathers will also get ruffled if it's molting or if it's unwell. It's a universally accepted truth in the scientific community that birds don't like it when their feathers are ruffled by another bird or—in captivity—by a person.

Just like birds, we can experience ruffled feathers for many reasons. God sometimes allows the ruffling because He needs us to clean up some part of our lives. He can also use the ruffling to turn up the heat, drawing us closer to Him for warmth. Ruffled feathers can also be a symptom of some other problem. And we don't like it when our feathers are ruffled any more than a bird does.

Yet we can see purpose in the feathers. Even purpose in the ruffles. Sometimes God smooths the feathers. Sometimes He lets the ruffles grow us. Always, He loves us through it all.

Chapter One

Self-inflicted Ruffling

Rhonda

I would kick this chapter off by pointing out how funny it is when we ruffle our feathers, except that it's not all that funny. Not funny at all actually. I've done it. I wonder how many times I've gotten myself into an unnecessary ruffle kerfuffle. If getting worked up were a workout, I would be in a lot better shape.

Physically, while I may not stick with an exercise plan well, if I got points for all the plans I've started, I would have some serious points. Not aerobic points. Just points. I'm in with the gym membership. Then out. In. Out. In. Out. At least it sounds aerobic. Still, I am the Hokey-Pokey of gym members.

I confess, most of the time I'm all too flex when it comes to what I label as "my workout." Presently, I've "turned myself around," and I'm back in at the gym. This time I started gradually, just like I read I should. So for the first week or so, I spent several minutes thinking about yoga pants. Intently.

Step Counting

My work out a few days ago was pretty awesome, though. First, I spent 20 minutes walking all over the house looking for my car keys so I could drive to the gym. I counted that. Then after I got there, I spent 20 more minutes trying to untangle my earphones. Counted that, too. Because, hey, I was at the gym. By that time, I only had about 10 minutes left, and I spent that showering. Workout? Check.

Today's exercise routine was a bit more intense, but I didn't do it at the gym. I call it the "there was a sock behind the dryer" workout, and I think I was actually sweating this time. Plus, I later burned more than 2000 calories—meaning I left a can of cinnamon rolls in the oven too long. Working out is hard. Sometimes ruffling.

Paul gives us some interesting workout instructions when he says to "work out your salvation" in Philippians 2:12. He's not talking about working *for* our salvation. I wonder if his statement ruffled some feathers back in his day. Because we see clearly in God's Word that Jesus did all the work that was needed for our salvation when He died on the cross for us. Salvation is complete. So how can we *work it out*?

Working Out/Working In

The instruction here actually is to allow what's already *in* to show up on the *out*. It's about obedience and steering away from sin. "So then, my dear friends, just as you have always obeyed, not only in my presence, but now even more in my absence, work out your salvation with fear and trembling" (Philippians 4:12 HCSB). The *how* is answered in the next verse: "For it is God who is working in you, enabling you both to desire and to work out His good purpose" (Philippians 2:13 HCSB).

Workout? Check! His good purpose works its way from the inside out, smoothing out those ruffles, as we grow in obedience, and as we lean into His power.

Sometimes difficulties and challenges are not the result of anything wrong we've done personally. It's the way of life in a fallen world. But how many times do we whine and complain about a ruffle that *is* a direct result from a bad choice we've made?

Let's own up to some of those ruffles, confess any sin and get it out of the way so we can walk in fruitful, God-honoring faith. It's a huge part of living unruffled. The goal should always be to take an active role in our spiritual growth and allow the Father to mature us by staying spiritually engaged. There are no points for spiritual couch potatoes.

This Workout Ain't for Wimps

Allowing the Lord to work in us does not mean our growth will never be a bit strenuous. Sometimes working out is hard. Allowing Him to work through us in building His church, continuing consistently in prayer, loving on His people and serving them even when they're contrary, and staying disciplined in reading His Word—it's not always the easiest. But it's the sweet place of satisfaction and joy—and it's oh so anti-ruffling.

On top of that, there's the wonderful news that God will spark our hearts and our desires and change what we want. Outside of Christ, we are only, ever and always a tangled feather-mess. God gives us the ability to unruffle, yes, but even more, as we trust in Him, He grants us "both to desire and to work out" His calling. There's blessed victory in seeing the Lord work it out—doing in and through us what we once couldn't bring ourselves even to desire without His Holy Spirit making it happen. That's growth. And it's a growth that smooths feathers we've ruffled, prevents further ruffling, and brings glory to the Father. Never mind what happens with the workout at the gym, because in the Hokiest-Pokiest terms, glory to the Father—*that's* what it's all about.

In Step—Two, Three, Four—with Jesus

By the way, on the other, *other* side of working out physically (wait, how many sides can there be?), you might be glad to hear that I'm not one to include dancing like nobody is watching in my fitness routine. I've read the memes. But I don't do it. Mostly because I don't want to watch it either. I do, however, sing loud. And big. And sometimes with motions. I don't dance like no one is watching, but I have been known to sing like I'm vacuuming.

A couple of months ago, I did accidentally bust a few new moves, but it was because a bug flew into my hair. Talk about ruffled. And about weird choreography. Embarrassing, sure. I didn't even know I had those moves. A couple of my kids saw it, as a matter of fact, and then they begged me to put those moves away and never pull them out again. It was worth the bug in the hair just for that.

I heard it was Charles Baudelaire who said, "Dancing is poetry with arms and legs." He obviously never saw my moves. Either that or he was super bad at poetry. So hold on, Charles. Sorry, but this could be one more little proof that we can't believe everything we hear.

Would You Believe It?

When it comes to living unruffled, we can't believe everything we hear there either. Sometimes we welcome spirit-ruffles by listening to and believing untruths. Those who don't follow Christ will tell you that if you do all your stepping just so—if you have just the right look, the right family, the right houses and cars and things—if you have all the right moves in all the right places—then your life will be a graceful dance. Never a feather disturbed. They'll tell you that when you know the right people and can say the right words in the right way, that's when life will be good.

Sadly, you don't have to try the world's way for long before figuring out that those moves make up a dance that's everything awkward. It ends in embarrassment—and emptiness. Relying on comfort and wealth and power and self to make us happy will always end in that vacuum. With no singing.

How do we find the remedy for that emptiness, in the most graceful, spin-and-swing-and-whirl-of-joy way? Not in our culture. Not on our own.

Deruffling begins in the presence of truth. It burgeons in His Word. "Make my steps steady through Your promise; don't let any sin dominate me," (Psalm 119:133 HCSB). Our choice here? Let evil govern our steps. Or let the Lord.

"Through Your promise" means "by Your Word." And the indication in the original language is that the psalmist isn't actually talking about our sinful nature here, though that's a battle we never take lightly. But this refers to sinful influence. He's asking for deliverance from the dominance of evil people.

Where He Leads Me ...

All too often in life's dance, we take our cues from others who would love nothing more than to lead us off in some wrong direction. In that same psalm, we read, "I have kept my feet from every evil path to follow Your Word" (vs. 101 HCSB). The original language means "I hold back my feet." *Hold on, feet. Do the right thing.*

Our calling is to allow the Lord to work in and work out our salvation, to follow Him, and to give His Word a place of prominence. *Lord, lead us. In how we live in unruffled obedience, in how we think and act and live. Every single step.*

Feathering Your Nest

The opposite of ruffled? A huge facet of unruffled is peace.

> "Abundant peace belongs to those who love Your instruction; nothing makes them stumble" (Psalm 119:165 HCSB).

Loving His instruction and living in obedience makes the difference between peacefully and gracefully moving through a day, or stumbling and ruffling embarrassingly out of control. Poetry in motion or plummeting in an awkward commotion. Because seriously, some moves are never meant to be busted.

- How do you practically allow what's on the *in* to show up on the *out*?

- Have you prayed for friends or family who are victims of their own ruffling—believing lies, living in disobedience, not trusting God or His Word?

- If any of those friends or family asked you how they could move past all that, what would your counsel be? What Bible passages might you share?

Birds of a Feather—Together
From Edie

Rhonda's insight has certainly given my attitude a work out in this chapter! Ruffling my personal feathers is never my intention, but it happens way more often than I'd like. The heart-pounding stress it adds to my life is something I'm going to work harder to cut out of my routine. I'm not an exercise fan, but she outlines a routine I can add to my life. I'm definitely going to work harder to follow Christ's lead and leave the ruffling to others.

When I'm tempted to ruffle my feathers, Jesus, help me stop. Work out the frustration I feel by leading me into more peaceful paths.

Chapter *Two*

When Others Do the Ruffling

Edie

Sometimes the chaos that surrounds us comes directly from someone else. I'm an introvert, so there are days when being around others can increase my stress level. Add difficult people into the mix and instead of standing strong, I run for cover. Jesus encountered chaos generated from difficult people and emerged unscathed. Not only did He survive, He brought a covering of peace that changed the entire situation.

We see His ability to bring peace in so many places in the Bible, but the one that always stands out to me is when the woman was brought before Him after having been caught in the act of adultery. I can't imagine a more chaotic place and time. The woman must have been hysterical, knowing the fate that awaited her. The mob would have been full of righteous anger, hurling accusations and threats. The Pharisees would have been smug, ready to discredit Jesus no matter what He said.

Walking in Jesus' Example

And Jesus? He was perfectly at peace. He didn't engage. He didn't defend or argue. He bent down and wrote something in the dirt. Oh the speculation that has gone into what words he wrote. But *what* He wrote is ultimately unimportant. His actions are the key for us. We see Him remaining calm and doing the unexpected.

In this instance, we aren't specifically told He stopped and prayed, but we know He was always in constant contact with the Father through the Holy Spirit so we know prayer was part of it. Because of that strong connection, He could react outside the chaos—without being drawn into the fray. And before the event was finished, His peace reigned supreme.

I'm determined to let Him work the same miracle in my interactions with people who ruffle my feathers.

My personal encounters with difficult people haven't always gone smoothly. But I've learned a lot—even through the mistakes. Recently I was able to practice during a difficult situation. I was testifying against the man who murdered my best friend and her daughter ... for a second time.

Our Walk of Peace

As I walked into the courtroom, it was déjà vu in the worst sense of the word. In 2003 the husband of my best friend had been convicted of her murder and sentenced to life without parole. Now, after a mistrial had been declared, we got to do it all over again.

The prosecution team and I had spent several hours the previous evening going over what to expect. They'd warned me the defense would attempt to rip holes in my story and discredit me any way they could. I was cautioned about possible pitfalls and traps they'd probably set for me. My testimony was a small but vital part in making sure this man returned to jail. I was terrified. My feathers were anything but unruffled, and I left the meeting uncertain whether I'd be able to sleep at all that night.

Before I'd left to travel to Denver—where the trial was held—I'd taken some actions to help me through the ordeal. I enlisted people to pray for me—an entire team of folks storming the throne of Heaven on my behalf. I also talked over my fears with someone I trusted. I'd learned that keeping my fears secret would give them power. Bringing them into the light weakened them. Some of the fears I voiced were truly ridiculous when I said them out loud, but in my mind they'd been true terrors. Finally, I resolved to leave the results of my testimony and ultimately the trial in God's hands.

This last bit of preparation is the hardest, but I've found it's the most important when dealing with people who ruffle our feathers. You see, we can only—ultimately—control ourselves. We can't fix others. Nobody hates that not-in-control-feeling more than me. I'd love to go around with a personality dust rag and neaten up everyone else's rough edges. And there are many times I wish someone would do that for me.

So I spent some time on the phone that evening before bed—talking with those who were praying for me. Then I took time to read my Bible, journal my prayers, and once again turn the outcome over to God. I slept like a baby—no nightmares or anything to disturb my sleep.

The next morning, as I walked into the courtroom, an extraordinary calm surrounded me. My mind was clear, and I could almost physically feel the Holy Spirit walking beside me and settling in as I took the witness stand.

Sure enough, the defense pounced. As their lawyer questioned me, the traps they laid seemed obvious, and I was easily able to speak the truth without compromise. I was on the stand a little over an hour, but the time sped by. The covering of peace didn't waver, no matter the intensity of the attacks directed at me. As I left the stand, I felt sad because I could feel the almost-physical connection with God's Spirit begin to dissipate. Just like Peter on the mount of transfiguration, I wanted to pitch my tent and live in the place where I had experienced God like never before.

The prosecution held a short debrief with me, and they stated their amazement. Turns out after our meeting the night before they hadn't had high expectations for my testimony. But they were pleased and kept referring to the beautiful peace and calm that had surrounded me. I was able to tell them it was supernatural because it was God and God alone. They were hopeful for a positive outcome for the trial and sure enough, he was once again found guilty and sentenced to life without parole.

Living Out the Example

After that experience, I've been able to apply that peace it to all kinds of feather-ruffling situations.

- **When I encounter difficult people, I pray first.** I pray for the person who irritates me. I ask God to let me see them through His eyes. And if I can't love them, I ask Him to love them through me. I prayed for the lawyers in that trial, and I've prayed for years for the man who murdered my best friend. It was so hard to pray for him at first. I couldn't image a Heaven that allowed in the man who killed my friend. But God began to work in my heart, and I realized not only could Heaven be that place, it would be a victory party beyond belief. Someone who had done such a horrible crime becoming a new creature is powerful. So I still pray for that kind of transformation in his life every day.

- **I also enlist others to pray for me and for the situation.** In that instance, I could be specific about what was happening. But in other instances, being too open in our prayer requests can become gossip. When you find others to pray for and with you, make certain they'll pray without knowing the details.

- **Then I'll get wise counsel about the situation.** I've learned to find someone I can be completely honest with. I let them know all I'm feeling, positive as well as negative. Talking out the truth can shine light on the situation.

- **Finally, I turn the results over to God.** Sometimes I turn them over to Him minute-by-minute because I keep taking them back. At other times, I surrender the results and am able to walk away. I've learned to keep relinquishing control as often as necessary.

Feathering Your Nest

For each of us, there are times when our feathers are ruffled by others who haven't harmed us in a major way. Often my emotional equilibrium is tilted by someone who doesn't even mean to upset me. But these smaller upsets can have a big impact. We should never ignore them or minimize the affect they can have on us.

No matter how small or big, it's always important to regain our feathery equilibrium.

I tend to react better when I'm prepared. And while it's not always possible to prepare for unexpected chaos, we can carry an arsenal of God's Word with us and make a game plan for dealing with ruffly people. These are my go-to verses ready to pull out when feathers start ruffling:

> "I have said these things to you, that in me you may have peace. In the world you will have tribulation. But take heart; I have overcome the world" (John 16:33 ESV).

When we think about Christ overcoming the world, we often think of end times. But He has promised us abundance here and now. I believe we have to make a conscious decision to embrace that abundance. Here are some questions to consider.

- What does "Christ overcoming the world" mean for you today?

- Who in your life is ruffling your feathers? How can you pray for this specific situation and person?

- Do you have people in your life who can give you wise counsel? Make a list of those you trust who can help you sort out the truth of the situation your facing. Pray over the list and then approach one of them to be your wise counsel.

Birds of a Feather—Together
From Rhonda

Some poignant thoughts in this chapter, for sure. When faced with a choice whether I'm going to duck for cover, or choose to rest in Christ's peace covering, I wish I could tell you I always choose well. I love how Edie points us to His peace that reigns supreme. I want to determine right alongside her to allow Christ to work the same miracle in how I respond to people who ruffle my feathers.

Whether it's an enormously grave ruffle, or a simple, feathery annoyance, Jesus, please reign in me. All glory to You.

Chapter *Three*

Situational Ruffling

Rhonda

A lizard. In the house. On the bed.

I was housesitting for some friends when I was younger. I must not be all that good at housesitting, because there he was. A creepy-looking, scaly invader. How could I let it happen?

I confess, my initial response was sheer panic. Then for a split second, I found myself thinking about how to save 15% or more on car insurance. Then back to panic.

Personal statement of fact regarding how we (I) group living creatures: herd of cows, school of fish, pack of wolves, psychotic episode of lizards. My editor hates (really hates) all caps so I can't use them, but please understand that when I tell you the thing was in the house, the all caps is implied.

I also hope you didn't miss the part where I said he was on the bed. On the BED. Okay yes, journalistic integrity out the window. Unlike the lizard. Because he was indeed not out the window. He was *on the bed*. I went to find something large enough to use to shoo him out the nearest lizard-sized opening. When I got back, he was gone. And then so was I. Just kidding. I stayed. But I stayed carrying a bazooka. No, still kidding. It was a baseball bat.

I'll tell you right now, though, I was never—no, no, never—getting in that bed. Restless Lizard Syndrome. That's a thing.

By the way, when there's a lizard in the house and sleeping is not an option, I highly recommend a bag of Chips Ahoy. And I do mean the entire bag of Chips Ahoy.

I know what some of you are thinking. God's creatures and all that. I even agree. Except it's more challenging to remind myself to agree when I've seen a leviathan. On. The. Bed.

Scaling Up the Perspective

Still, in the house, on the bed, at work or church, or at the doctor's office—wherever and whenever there's a surprise ruffling challenge—I want to remind myself to agree with the truth of my God. When we remember who He is, we're readier for any and every challenge, big or small, scaly or unscaly. Through His work in us, we're able to respond in faith and courage.

In Psalm 55, David is in distress. In verse 2, he pleads with God, "Attend to me, and answer me; I am restless in my complaint and I moan." Restless Lizard Syndrome to the max. "My heart is in anguish within me; the terrors of death have fallen upon me. Fear and trembling come upon me, and horror overwhelms me" (v 4-5).

But David ends the chapter testifying, "But I will trust in you," (vs. 23) and in the verse right before it, he charges us: "Cast your burden on the Lord, and he will sustain you."

Past the Panic to the Plan and Purpose

Keeping our eyes on Him and our sights on eternity changes how we see challenges. Panic may be the first response. Our bodies and psyches are rather built that way. But we don't have to live in panic. After allowing ourselves a knee-jerk, we can head straight for His sustaining comfort. The God who indwells us is in control, loves us deeply, and holds our future in His hands. He will sustain us. He has a plan for us—a grand purpose—and it won't be thwarted.

When God spoke of the intimidating leviathan (Job 41), Job responded, "I know that you can do all things, and that no purpose of yours can be thwarted" (Job 42:2).

Our Creator is infinitely bigger and mightier than any challenge. He's got this. He's got you. His sustaining comfort really is all that and a bag of cookies. All the life-cookies, as a matter of fact. The better we know Him and understand His character—and the more we lean on Him—the better we're able to handle surprises, even the surprise of hardship, discomfort, and suffering.

Still, troubles shouldn't really catch us off guard. We need to be reminded often that we live in a sin-cursed world. Difficulties happen. We can let a tough situation ruffle us, or we can look to the Lord, trust what He says, and find strength even when we're in the toughest situations. Unexpected challenging situations, even the most difficult hot and fiery kind, do not have to steal our peace and ruffle our feathers.

Even When You Get Up on the Wrong Side of the Lizard

Peter experienced those challenges and trials first-hand, up close and personal-like. But God empowered and inspired Paul to write this encouragement for us, "Beloved, do not be surprised at the fiery trial when it comes upon you to test you, as though something strange were happening to you. But rejoice insofar as you share Christ's sufferings, that you may also rejoice and be glad when his glory is revealed," (1 Peter 4:12-13).

Don't be surprised. We should actually expect those unexpected ruffles. They can't touch our soul. And Peter takes it a step further. He encourages us to rejoice. As in, *find joy in,* the challenge. We can know Jesus and His glory even better through it.

Finding joy, singing through the difficult times, it might sound like a Christianese pat response to trials. Say it to your neighbor, and he might stare at you as if you were speaking some sort of spiritual-lizard-alien language. Yet we truly can experience peace and joy as we rest in the presence of Christ and plug in to His Word.

Soothing the Savage Me

By the way, before I learn to speak whatever that spiritual-lizard-alien language might be, I've wondered if I should try snake charming. Not on my neighbor, but with any subsequent reptiles I might encounter. OK, not really. But it did take me a few minutes to remember in that earlier lizard encounter that lizards don't understand the language of "Shriek." And that I do not speak Lizard.

Even so, I generally love languages. I recently took a look at some interesting dead languages. You know, like Latin, Ancient Egyptian, Sanskrit, Comic Sans, and Cursive.

Ah, cursive. Remember that? I was actually fluent in Cursive at one at one time. My kids still ask me why we ever had it. Anytime they ask, I get a little defensive and act all hoity-toity and superior, but I only do it to distract them from the fact that I don't actually have a real answer.

It's fascinating to me that while some languages languish, new ones burgeon. For instance, I'm still trying to learn to speak "Laundry." According to the hieroglyphs they now use, I'm pretty sure I have to wash at least a couple of new shirts inside the royal crown of Denmark and dry them in some sort of crop circle. What's especially weird is that I don't even remember leaving this planet to buy these shirts.

Language barriers—lizard, laundry, and otherwise—are challenging. Especially when you run into them out of the blue. I ordered a blender not long ago, and the entire instruction booklet was in Korean. I finally figured out how to make a smoothie, but probably only because I was already studying to learn the language of Laundry. I guess glyphs are glyphs. My smoothie did taste a little like liquid Tide, but maybe that's just me.

The Unruffled Language of Truth

I never want to be unaware of barriers that can interrupt a fruit-filled faith walk though. The last action we want to take is to invite foolish philosophies in to ruffle our thought lives. Those errant philosophies are sneaky. They know how to speak our language, as it were. Like that line of thinking mentioned in chapter one: right look, right family, right house, right car, right possessions—get those and then life is sweet and easy and everything will be ... right.

It's the kind of thinking that can creep into our thought patterns before we notice, maybe even hindering our capacity to receive actual truth. Sometimes we do notice counterfeits creeping in, so we let them soak there for a bit. We may catch ourselves listening to the world's foolish thoughts so often and for so long that fake starts to sound right to us.

That's one more reason we need to stay committed to making God's Word part of our everyday—our deepest heart-language. I doubt we could ever overemphasize the importance of His Word. It makes its way through barriers of folly and fluff, exposing them as the foolishness they are. We're told in Proverbs 15:14 that "The heart of him who has understanding seeks knowledge, but the mouths of fools feed on folly." That folly diet? No thanks. Tastes worse than any laundry soap.

Just as a steady diet of laundry detergent would leave a bubbly-bad taste in our mouths, constantly feeding our minds and hearts on all kinds of media that is contrary to God's Word will put up a barrier between us and the truth, giving us a skewed view of right and wrong, inviting soul-ruffles we don't want or need. That's when unreasonable fear, hoity-toity pride, silly doubt—and a long list of other negatives—color our decisions and hinder our joy and our ability to live the unruffled life of faith. All those who deny the truth and malign the wisdom of God and His Word are simply not speaking our language.

Ruffles Come A-tumbling Down

Barriers crumble against God's Word. His Word guards our hearts from the ruffling. The Bible teaches the language of wise, pure living. "How can a young man keep his way pure? By guarding it according to your Word. I have stored up your Word in my heart, that I might not sin against you" (Psalm 119:9, 11).

There's a life-changing message there, in any language. It's a message of peace. You might actually call it the language of Unruffled.

Let's commit to learning His language well—with everything we've got. His grace will get us through, His Word will be our guide. A surprise challenge, an unexpected leviathan—they don't have to ruffle our feathers. Or our scales.

Feathering Your Nest

An eternal perspective makes all the difference. It doesn't always take away every stinging pain or the initial shock of an unexpected difficulty. But when we hold that difficulty up against the light of a glorious eternity, our worst leviathans are still "light" and "momentary."

> "Therefore we do not become discouraged [spiritless, disappointed, or afraid]. Though our outer self is [progressively] wasting away, yet our inner self is being [progressively] renewed day by day. For our momentary, light distress [this passing trouble] is producing for us an eternal weight of glory [a fullness] beyond all measure [surpassing all comparisons, a transcendent splendor and an endless blessedness]! So we look not at the things which are seen, but at the things which are unseen; for the things which are visible are temporal [just brief and fleeting], but the things which are invisible are everlasting and imperishable" (2 Corinthians 4:16-18, AMP).

✒ Spend some time meditating and thanking God for your "everlasting and imperishable" "endless blessedness." Consider writing about your contemplation in a journal or post about it as a testimony and encouragement to your friends and family. Or hey, send *me* a message.

✒ Even the strongest, most mature Jesus followers can be a little rattled by a difficult surprise. If you're still in that initial startled panic of a tough situation, remind your heart and your head of what is true. Your God is loving and strong and kind and good. He will comfort you.

✒ Find that comfort and amazing renewal by spending time alone with your heavenly Father every day this week—difficult circumstances or no difficult circumstances. Encounter Him, especially at the beginning of your day.

How can that kind of encounter change how you face any ruffling "unexpecteds" you might face?

Birds of a Feather—Together
From Edie

I don't mind lizards—outside—with lots of room around me to run. Sharing a bed with one would definitely be a feather-ruffling proposition. But as scary as that would be, Rhonda reminds us there are other instances when we need the protection of Jesus. Whether we're facing a scaly invader or something more immense, Jesus is always bigger. In any situation His answers are the unruffling kind that vanquish all scary—scaly—invaders. The reminder that Jesus speaks peace into every panic-filled circumstance is a message I can incorporate into my life.

Banishing panic with peace is Your gift. Help us react to life's unwelcome surprises by running to You and letting You speak peace into the things that ruffle.

Chapter *Four*

Smoothing Emotional Ruffles

Edie

I really hate to admit it, but I am an emotional person. I would like to think of myself as a well-balanced, thoughtful person who is never driven to act by an emotional whim. But that's not always an accurate picture of who I am—it's rarely who I am. And while being aware of my emotions isn't a bad thing, it *can* lead me to spontaneous acts of love and generosity. However, emotions can also lead me into trouble if I allow negative emotions to command my thoughts and actions. This detrimental turn in the path is especially true when I've been hurt.

Emotional wounds occur in irregular patterns. We can be hurt by the thoughtlessness of others, by circumstances, and by loss. These emotional injuries can lead us to act in unpleasant ways and say words we wouldn't normally say. Emotional bruises can even dominate our thoughts to such an extent that we go places in our minds we'd never go otherwise. Emotionally ruffled feathers are sometimes the hardest to sooth.

Unruffling Emotions

So where do we go to unruffle our feathers? The obvious answer is God. And while that's also the right answer, sometimes it's not so black and white. Soothing emotional ruffles is often tied to two actions—forgiving and moving on.

When I revel in the fact that my feathers are in a ruffle. I'm like a male peacock, strutting his plumage for all the world to see. I want everyone to see my beautiful—offended—feathers. Why? Because it feels good to have the sympathy of others, and when the ruffling is caused by someone else, wallowing in the pain is a way to get back at them.

Conversely, when I take my hurt to God, He takes it away. Ultimately that's always good. But I'm a slow learner and sometimes it takes me a while to get to the point where I *want* Him to take away the hurt.

That happened when I found out my friend's husband had murdered her. I was coldly, unforgivably angry. I was mad at God, at my friend, and especially mad at her husband. I didn't want to forgive, I wanted to see vengeance. I called it justice, but in truth I wanted much more than judgment.

Embracing Unruffling ... No Matter What

Allowing God to unruffle my feathers about that incident was abhorrent to me. I wanted to hate him—and I wanted everyone else to hate him too. My friend was gone and her killer was still alive—and doing his best to avoid the consequences of his actions. This was a circumstance I didn't think I could live with.

I realize that you might be irritated that I'd bring up such an extreme example. Because really, if I can forgive someone like this, then I've pretty much taken away excuses to hold onto ruffled feathers about other offenses. Believe me, even with that kind of an obstacle in my past, I still struggle with emotionally ruffled feathers. And each instance of ruffling hurts. Do not make the mistake of trivializing your emotional pain. Sometimes the oddest situations wound us deeply.

Small Steps . . . Big God

One lesson this experience taught me was that God could—and would—take the time to smooth my feathers. It also taught me to walk in steps . . . small steps. That was the case with my friend's murderer.

The first step to begin the healing process of forgiving him was to pray. I couldn't start off praying God would forgive this man. Instead I backed up and asked God to change my heart enough to allow me to pray for God to help me forgive him.

I prayed this small prayer resentfully at first, because I knew it was the right thing. Not because he deserved forgiveness, but because I deserved closure. I must have prayed this one prayer for almost a year before I could move on to the next step. *Yes, sometimes I'm a really slow learner.*

My next prayer was for God to show me how forgiveness expressed itself if lived out. I had to know what God expected of me if I forgave the man. I was deeply afraid that my healing would involve some kind of confrontation with this man.

God didn't download a movie of what a soul-to-soul life would be like when I began to walk in forgiveness. Instead God asked me to trust Him. Trust was hard. I felt like I'd trusted Him with my friend and look what happened there. I know that was the wrong attitude, but this is the struggle I had, and I can't change it.

God's Word is clear that He loves us and wants to bless us, but it sure didn't feel like blessing. During these dark days, I gripped God's Word, trying to make sense of this senseless situation. "For I know the plans I have for you, declares the Lord, plans for welfare and not for evil, to give you a future and a hope" (Jeremiah 29:11 ESV). I returned to this verse again and again. Finally I dug deep into the circumstances and meaning around this passage and the light began to dawn.

Living in God's Plan

The Israelites were in exile, and Jeremiah was confronting the false prophet, Hananiah. Hananiah claimed God was going to free the nation from Babylon in two years. God didn't bring freedom on Hananiah's time-table and commanded Jeremiah to set the record straight. God had a different plan for Israel. He was teaching them to flourish in the midst of suffering. He was promising the ability thrive in the midst of difficult situations.

Suffering and difficulty was where I was.

No amount of justice was going to bring my friend back. I needed to learn how to thrive in the midst of this grief and anger. The only way to do that was by following the path of forgiveness.

As my heart softened, God began to speak to me. He reminded me of my friend's ardent prayers on behalf of her husband before she died. I knew—in my heart of hearts—that she would be rejoicing if this man could accept Christ and walk through the gates of Heaven. God showed me that wouldn't be unfair, it would be *victory*. Someone unforgivable would have been transformed into a new creation.

With this new vision of what forgiveness meant, I began to pray for God to change my heart, and He did. This forgiveness didn't involve any contact with this man, and I'm grateful. God showed me that forgiveness doesn't mean putting myself back in a bad situation. He's fine with boundaries, as long as I consult Him for guidance.

I've discovered that boundaries don't inhibit or confine my prayers. I pray for the man who murdered my friend and their daughter daily, asking God to reach his heart and change him. But the most important part of this forgiveness has been the change in me. I have a much deeper understanding of what God's forgiveness looks like. It's made me quicker to forgive smaller offenses, once I get past the emotion of being hurt.

Showing My Ruffles

Now when I'm faced with emotional ruffled feathers, I take them to God asking Him to show me the emotional root of my upheaval. I'm honest about my feelings and my fears. He already knows what's going on in my heart, but I have to take that honest look at myself so I can hear what God has to say.

I give myself permission to take the smoothing process slowly. Sometimes it's baby steps, sometimes I can stride right into forgiveness. But it takes as long as it takes.

I refuse to return to the initial hurt and rehash it after I've taken the step of forgiveness. This can be difficult if something similar happens again.

With God's guidance, I set healthy boundaries. I haven't contacted the man who murdered my friend and their daughter and have no plans to contact him in the future. I have complete peace from God about that decision, and I'm walking in that peace.

Feathering Your Nest

Where are you with the whole emotional ruffling? I've found that when God brings up a new concept or reminds me of one I already know, it's time to do some self-examination. Most of the time there's something in my life that needs re-adjusting. But sometimes, He shares insight so I can be prepared to speak truth into someone else's life. These revelations come in many ways. There are the normal channels—reading the Word, prayer and godly counsel. But more often insights sneak up on me. They occur to me while I'm doing something else, or through an overheard conversation.

Ponder what to do when our emotional feathers are ruffled.

- When you consider Jeremiah 29:11, what hope do you need to move past what has happened? Be honest. God will meet you where you are—without condemnation—even if it's in the middle of anger and unforgiveness.

- What part of this situation requires you to forgive yourself? In my case, I had to forgive myself for not seeing the abuse that was taking place in my friend's marriage. It was well-hidden and even though I didn't know, I was terribly angry with myself.

- How do I need to change my prayers to move past this emotional situation?

- What boundaries—if any—do I need to put into place to continue to stay emotionally healthy?

Birds of a Feather—Together
From Rhonda

On a microscopic level compared to what Edie experienced, I struggled with an offense. I had taught women all over the country that harboring bitterness would darken their lives, hurt marriages, and spill over onto their children, affecting every relationship. I told them food doesn't even taste as good when there is unforgiveness. Though I'd taught it for years, never was it more real to me than when I experienced it firsthand. It took me several months to forgive. And I have to tell you, those were rotten months. It renewed my fervor to not keep a tab when it comes to others' sins against me.

Jesus, may I focus on the forgiveness You offered me. May it reflect in my every other relationship. In Your name.

Part Two:
More Faith, Less Fluff

All birds have several different types of feathers, and each one is necessary and serves a purpose. The *pinions* or *wing* feathers are straight and strong, enabling flight. There are also *tail* feathers, and shorter *contour* feathers. In addition, there are *down* and *semiplume* feathers.

These fluffy feathers help a bird regulate body heat. This is particularly important to waterfowl like geese and penguins who live in cold climates. The down is critical to trapping body heat.

But down can't provide warmth working alone. If a bird were just covered in this light and airy feather, it wouldn't be able to repel moisture. These feathers are delicate and wouldn't prevent the accumulation of dirt and parasites, or prevent injury. Downy fluff is good, but only when it's protected below a covering of stronger, contour feathers.

Faith is like that. It's that covering that keeps us protected from all kinds of attack at the soul level. As we enter times of ruffling—and we all do—it's good to understand that trouble does not have to ruffle our souls. Not even a little.

Chapter *Five*

Examples of Living Unruffled in the Bible

Edie

I love how relevant and real the Bible is. God's Word doesn't sugar coat life. He uses authentic—flawed—people to illustrate His truth, His forgiveness, and His grace. I see a composite of myself in almost everyone I read about. I'm an occasional Mary and an all-too-often Martha clone. I'm as impulsive as Peter, as much of a doubter as Thomas, and as unwilling to leave circumstances in God's capable hands as Sarah.

Some days I'm not certain living unruffled is a possibility for someone as flawed as me. Anytime life throws me a curve, I get my feathers in a kerfuffle. For example, there was a trip I took to speak at a conference when several of my appliances staged a full-scale revolt. I wasn't there, but my poor husband and three sons witnessed the carnage.

The first I heard about the disaster was a call from my husband. He announced, via cell phone, that our refrigerator had died. Yes, he'd called the repair man before he called me—he's a truly wise man—but all the technician could do was apply a temporary fix so I could be the one to pick out the new one once I got home. The next day hubby called again. This time the casualty was our clothes dryer, and it was beyond help.

On the last day of my conference I was leaving a class when my phone vibrated in my pocket. Sure enough, the picture on the screen promised it was my beleaguered husband. I seriously considered letting it go to voice mail, but my better nature prevailed, and I worked up the fortitude to answer. Sure enough our stove and microwave—two separate appliances in our home—had joined the list of dead and dying devices.

Seeing Jesus' Example

On the flight home God and I had a discussion.

I began by pointing out to Him that while I was away from home being obedient, He could at least look after the homefront. I reminded Him how hard it was to concentrate on what He wanted me to do when my life was in upheaval. Surely He could orchestrate better circumstances from now on.

He should have thumped me hard on the head. But instead of sending down a lightning bolt at my audacity, I felt a nudge in my spirit that brought to mind several passages I'd studied in the past. I could hear the whispered words of a former pastor in my mind, "All the answers to life are found in Jesus." Could it really be true— even in the mundane battles I was facing? I decided to begin there and set out to study Jesus during the chaotic years of His ministry.

As I reread the accounts of Jesus' three short years of ministry I was reluctant to see Him as a legitimate example. I tried explaining to the Creator of the Universe, Jesus was God so He had the ability to stay unruffled. I was flawed and weak. I needed my heavenly Father to cut me some slack.

We are never so blind as when we refuse to see.

I deserved to have my feathers plucked. I read on, "Truly, truly, I say to you, whoever believes in me will also do the works that I do; and greater works than these will he do, because I am going to the Father" (John 14:12 ESV).

Even if I could ignore how well Jesus handled ministry in real life circumstances, I couldn't minimize the fact that we are also promised the ability to do His great works. Not because we're now self-sufficient—never that. Instead it was possible because we have a helper. Jesus sent us the Holy Spirit to provide everything we needed and more.

Avoiding the Trap

I was out of excuses.

I recognized that I'd fallen into the trap of dismissing how Jesus lived simply because I knew He was the Son of God. I completely ignored that Jesus was also fully human—struggling with weariness, stress, and the difficulties of balancing life. He faced the same issues we face today—difficult family situations and members, drama from His friends and followers, and a world that was hostile. I relate to all these frustrations.

After apologizing to God and asking forgiveness, I spent the next few weeks looking at Jesus' life. I dissected and devoured every encounter the Bible records and translated it into a pattern I could apply to my life. We must never make the mistake of trivializing the trials He faced. Within those trials lay the keys to living unruffled in the midst of chaos.

Learning from the Master

Jesus' actions flowed from the relationship He had with His Father. Just like us, He and His Father shared a yoke as He served. He didn't try to do anything apart from God. His strength was not His own. It flowed from the power of God at work through Him.

Jesus' life was characterized by an ongoing conversation with God. In the Word, I saw instances where the specific communication was spelled out and other instances where the conversations between Jesus and the Father were referred to or implied. Regardless, staying in touch with the Father was a defining hallmark of the way Jesus lived.

Jesus' priorities were following God's path, no matter how difficult. He didn't allow the expectations of others dictate His actions or distract Him from the purpose of God.

Another Example

I wanted to see if these principles were modeled elsewhere in the Bible. So I turned to Judges in the Old Testament and another of my favorite people—Deborah. Even though we don't know a lot about her history, we do get enough to see a wonderful example of living unruffled. "Now Deborah, a prophetess, the wife of Lappidoth, was judging Israel at that time (Judges 4:4 ESV).

These few words may seem like a bare-bones sort of introduction, but it gives us a lot. We know that in her day and time, leadership positions weren't usually open to women. Because she was designated as a prophet as well as a judge, we know that leadership was spiritual as well as civic. We also learn she was a wife with all the duties associated with that position. For any of us who have tried to juggle work and home, we know her life was anything but placid. And yet she carried out her duties with calm authority.

Deborah handled one specific crisis when the nation was under the rule of Jabin. He was a powerful enemy and had a force of 900 iron chariots. God sent word through her that He would use Barak to break the oppression of Jabin. She delivered the message to Barak and instead of rejoicing, he balked. He insisted that he'd only follow God's direction if she was with him.

Can't you imagine her sigh at his response? I certainly can. In addition to her duties as a wife and judge, here was one more duty on her plate—and all because this man wouldn't follow God's direction. Of course that is all my interpretation. We aren't told she reacted like that. But I can't help but place myself in her shoes and imagine how I would feel.

We don't see any sign of ruffled feathers in this woman. Not a hint of frustration or even a lecture for Barak on his lack of faith. All we see is her unruffled acceptance of his terms—along with the admonition that he wouldn't be granted the glory of the victory. If that's not unruffled in the midst of chaos, I don't know what is.

Feathering Your Nest

Looking at biblical examples of unruffled lives is fundamental to learning to live with beautifully smooth feathers. We must never fall into the trap of believing our unruffled state is due to circumstances. Instead, we must look past the surface to see the power of God at. Ponder these powerful ideas to learn how to carry a core of peace.

When we turn to the Bible for inspiration we can find two types of instruction—the right way and the wrong way to live out God's truth.

✒ With this in mind, consider your favorite Bible stories. How do the people you read about help you learn more about living unruffled?

✒ Read again John 14:12. It can seem almost like blasphemy to consider doing more than Jesus Himself. But God's Word *never* lies. Look past the uncomfortable truth and consider God's amazing accomplishments through you thus far because you have the power of the Holy Spirit with you.

✒ As you think about Deborah and her situation, ponder the obstacles she must have faced when God appointed her to judge Israel. What are some similarities to your life now? How can you learn from her apply some of her unruffledness to your daily challenges?

Birds of a Feather—Together
From Rhonda

Every once in a while, trouble hits me right in the machinery—just as it did with Edie. Ouch. If I run to the Father, knowing He is faithful to work in me, I can respond honorably. He empowers that. Sometimes I actually get to see Him at work—right there in the heart of me—through those situations. Do I have to admit how many times instead of responding honorably, I respond onerably? It doesn't matter if that's not a real word, it's my real response.

Thank you for the reminders through the Bible that You can use the orneriest. Oh, the realness and relevance of His Word for my life!

Chapter *Six*

Faith that Shows Up, No Matter the Ruffles

Rhonda

Not that I'm big on throwing my time away, because I had plans for accomplishing something great today. But you have to understand, that video said I wouldn't *believe* what happened next. "BELIEVE"—it was in all caps just like that. It's not like I had a choice anyway, but I could see that this video had a baby in it. And a puppy. Only a monster could just scroll down like it wasn't a baby and a puppy.

There may have been a few other activities I squeezed onto the day's itinerary that didn't exactly start out there. However, those makeup tips on Pinterest are not going to pin themselves. And also, that word game on my phone keeps my brain sharp. Probably. Who needs a mind-sharpener more than I do? I've finger-swiped a lot of words in that game. Miles. I'm sure that's why my mind is a steel trap. I can't explain how the otter got in the trap. But still, I do think every now and then I hear him hollering, "YOLO!" It's about as cute as a puppy. But not cuter than a puppy and a baby.

YOLO? Well, Yes and No

Of course, that "You Only Live Once" philosophy is not all that biblically sound. Frittering my time away isn't any too biblical—even if my brain-otter says it's okay. At the end of this life, I wonder how many of us will say, "Sure wish I'd played more dragon games on my computer." Or maybe, "If only I'd spent more time looking at my phone."

It's not that recreation is a bad thing. There's often restful, rejuvenating purpose in a couple of kick-back-and-relax items on the itinerary. Knowing when to rest can keep the ruffles away. But we do only live once here. We need to spend our fleeting time wisely. I think if someone translated "YOLO" into Latin, it would be, "carpe diem." Every day is one that's begging to be seized.

Despite its familiarity, I still read Romans 12:1-2 regularly.

> "I appeal to you therefore, brothers, by the mercies of God, to present your bodies as a living sacrifice, holy and acceptable to God, which is your spiritual worship. Do not be conformed to this world, but be transformed by the renewal of your mind, that by testing you may discern what is the will of God, what is good and acceptable and perfect."

Though I read it routinely, it never fails to inspire me to seize the day. It does for my heart so much more than any word game could ever do for my brain. It's like a heart-soul-and-mind-sharpener.

Renewed by Remembering His Calling

When I allow Him and His Word to be my mind-sharpener, change happens. It's a renewing of mind that doesn't simply result in a nice word score, but one that can reveal "what is the will of God, what is good and acceptable and perfect." There's simply nothing I want out of this one and only physical life more than I want to know and do His will.

Live once in the physical—sure, YOLO. But for those of us who've been born again, life here is followed by an eternity spent in the glorious presence of Christ. Every time we think of that glory, we're inspired all the more to live each day like it's our last, loving Him with every minute we're given.

We can experience joy and peace in His call to rest. We can experience joy and peace in His call to get busy. The key is in our surrender, and in our reliance solely on Him for whatever it is that His calling … well … *calls* for.

Faith flourishes when we do that. Flourishes. Matures. Expands. Fluffs. It's the good kind of fluffing that really can de-ruffle a spirit.

On the Other Side of the Fluff

I'm not sure why, but there's a different type of fluffing, back on the physical side of life—and it's anything but the flourishing kind. I accidentally put one of my favorite "lay flat to dry" sweaters in the dryer. Somewhere in the last fluff cycle, somebody must've slipped in and traded it for some kind of little teddy bear sweater. Fluffed? That's a big nope. And now what am I supposed to do with this sweater? I guess now I have to buy a little teddy bear.

I've heard the same about invisibility cloaks. People don't tell you not to machine dry those things. Or maybe it's on the label. But reading an invisible label is not easy. I'm guessing with just the wrong fluff you end up with an invisibility *hanky*.

Since the introduction of machines for washing and drying, most of us have experienced mystic laundry in some realm or another. The proof? Socks. Scary things happen to socks. One. At. A. Time.

I don't go for that magical stuff, so I wouldn't know black magic from any other color, but I do know that you should always separate your darks from your lights.

Faith that Shows Up

In the spiritual realm, it's still advisable to separate dark from light. *O heavenly Father, may I live in uninterrupted, growing, unruffled faith in Jesus, the Light of the world.*

I really do want a faith that shows up. Visible. Large enough that everyone knows it's never been tumble-dried. Isn't it interesting that when the disciples asked Jesus to give them a large faith in Luke 17:5, Jesus answered, "If you had faith like a grain of mustard seed, you could say to this mulberry tree, 'Be uprooted and planted in the sea,' and it would obey you." Again in Matthew 17:20, we see where Jesus said, "If you have faith like a grain of mustard seed, you will say to this mountain, 'Move from here to there,' and it will move, and nothing will be impossible for you."

You could tumble dry faith—even on the perma-press cycle—and it would still be the perfect size to accomplish enormous feats. Impossible feats. It's not about the size of the faith. It's all about where the faith is placed. Faith in Jesus and obedience to His lordship. That's what separates the dark life from real life in the light. And in the light, faith becomes so beautifully visible.

"Now faith is the assurance of things hoped for, the conviction of things not seen. For by it the people of old received their commendation. By faith we understand that the universe was created by the Word of God, so that what is seen was not made out of things that are visible" (Hebrews 11:1-3). God created everything we see and everything we don't. Every time we ponder His creative power and remember that there is nothing in the universe too hard for Him, our faith grows. And our ability to live unruffled grows in like proportions.

Paul tells us in Romans 10:17 that faith comes by hearing and hearing by the Word of God. As we study our Creator through His Word and learn more about His power, His character, His trustworthiness, His love and His mercy, our faith grows yet more. We find new confirmation that He is all we need. It's the setting for a strong faith—one that everyone around can see. Gloriously visible.

That. Yes, that, we can *believe*.

Feathering Your Nest

The apostles walked, talked, ate, slept, and ministered alongside Jesus day in and day out. And they, *they*, had to ask the Lord to increase their faith. How much more should we? How would it change your today if you stopped right now and asked Him to grant you a big, growing, glorious, humongous faith—one visible to everyone you encounter today?

"For everyone born of God is victorious and overcomes the world; and this is the victory that has conquered and overcome the world—our [continuing, persistent] faith [in Jesus the Son of God]" (1 John 5:4 AMP).

🪶 The passage in 1 John reminds us that a continuing, persistent faith results in victory, and in overcoming the world. There's nothing more unruffling in this life. And as children of God, this victory is ours. In what areas could you use some victory? How can you claim it?

🪶 The passage also reminds us that Jesus has already done the overcoming. What does that do to our attitudes about living unruffled, and about living each day as if it's our last?

🪶 Called to rest? Rest. Called to get to work? Get to work. What is the key to having the ability to know which one to do, and the key to having the ability to do it?

Birds of a Feather—Together
From Edie

Fluff and stuff. Too often that's my answer to wash and wear faith. But faith isn't meant to be squished down out of sight and hoarded against a future need. It's meant to be used every day. Jesus has provided the life-softening additive of His presence that never loses its ability to soothe. As Rhonda so aptly shares, it should cover our lives like fine feathers—beautiful, insulating and impervious to ruffling.

When life gives us ruffles, remind us to turn to You and let You replace our washed out faith with one that endures.

Chapter Seven

How Does Unruffled Show Up Today

Edie

For years I hated mirrors.

I use them daily to check my hair and put on makeup. I couldn't avoid them, but viewed them as a necessary evil. I also have several decorative mirrors hanging in my house. They're gifts and I couldn't bring myself to hide them away in a closet, but they weren't presents I enjoyed. As you have already guessed, it wasn't the mirrors, I loathed, it was what I saw reflected in them that I despised.

I took great care to position each mirror above eye level—my eye level. I'm short, only about five-foot-one, so I thought my deception went unnoticed. Until the day my husband asked me why all the mirrors in the house were hung so high.

I'd been caught. I took a deep breath and confessed that when I caught sight of my reflection, dissatisfaction and an overwhelming sense of failure flooded my soul. At my answer I saw compassion and love in his eyes. That softened his next comment. "I think you need to figure out where this lie is coming from and how to get rid of it."

His observation sent me on a journey.

I've always struggled with my weight, and giving birth to three sons had made it worse. However, I couldn't blame my current obesity on genetics or metabolism or anything else. I knew the cause of my weight gain was eating too much, eating the wrong things, and not being active enough. But those factors weren't the root of my ruffled self-image. The foundation of the problem was that I had believed a lie. I had invited it into my soul and embraced it as truth.

Difficult Insight

Even armed with my husband's insight, it took a while for me to discover the lie embedded in my heart. As I prayed through this situation, I heard the echo of a woman's comment and realized where this debilitating self-image had come from.

She was an acquaintance at church. Although many years have passed, I can recall the circumstances like they were yesterday. I stood with a group of women and she remarked she could never trust a speaker or author who was overweight. I did my best not to react, but shame flooded my soul. She explained her reasoning—if someone couldn't manage their physical discipline well enough to stay in shape, they couldn't be relied on to handle the Word of God accurately.

I ducked my head, certain everyone in the group was looking at me. As far as I know, no one else gave her words further thought. I was too embarrassed to ask anyone else's perspective on the conversation. Instead, I absorbed that comment, assumed it was true, and didn't bother to measure it against God's Word. After that, even though God was throwing open doors for my speaking and writing, I felt no joy.

Who is Sabotaging You?

I had allowed the enemy to use her words to sabotage the call God had put on my life. Somehow I accepted the lie that for God to use me, I must have every aspect of my life perfectly together. Nothing could be farther from the truth. God doesn't use us because we are perfect. He uses us because He loves us.

That was the truth I'd so easily discarded.

I was judging my ability to be used by God on *my ability* ... not His. And not trusting Him was affecting my life. I couldn't find peace in what God was doing through me because I had ingested a lie, allowed it to take root and choke out the truth.

What does this have to do with living unruffled? Quite a lot.

Being unruffled today—and every day—requires living from the inside out. It's a mindset that takes practice for it to become the default way of doing life. For me, it's become easier, but unless I'm paying attention, I can return to the practice of living life from the outside in. I'm still much too prone to letting my circumstances dictate my attitude—and the condition of my feathers.

The Weight of Circumstances

I'd allowed my circumstances to dictate my peace about my weight—and in the process—hinder how God wanted to use me. The perception I had of myself bled over into everything and kept my feathers in constant disarray. My distorted view rejected God's truth, "For we are his workmanship, created in Christ Jesus for good works, which God prepared beforehand, that we should walk in them" (Ephesians 2:10 ESV).

The lie I believed overshadowed the plan God had for me. My ruffles grew out of proportion, hindering my spiritual self with additional weight:

I hated being in front of people because I was ashamed of how my weight focused the spotlight on my lack of self-control. I believed everyone would discount what I said because they could see my lack of discipline in my size.

I avoided posing for pictures with friends and family and even at events because the images became a permanent record of my failure on display.

I struggled with the added burden of guilt when God opened doors for me, reasoning that others were more qualified and worthy.

I inspected every conversation for possible condemnation, and was quicker and quicker to take offense.

Ruffles Add Weight

Ruffled feathers make you look fat. No, seriously, I'm not joking. By letting my spiritual feathers poke out in all directions, I was reinforcing the lie I believed. Because I had discarded God's truth, I not only saw myself as physically fat, but also spiritually obese, out-of-control, undisciplined.

But what if your ruffled feathers have nothing to do with weight? Does any of this about believing lies apply? It does, because lies—all lies—are heavy burdens. Every ruffled feather distorts how we react to every situation, adding to the spiritual weight we carry. All the deceptions we accept as truth make us spiritually unhealthy.

The lies we believe reside deep inside us. Lies affect our hearts and poison our minds, breeding an infection that makes it harder and harder to experience all God has for us. When this kind of darkness invades our souls, it dries up the well of peace, and we have nothing to draw from when circumstances erupt.

Unruffled peace doesn't come because our circumstances are perfect or our lives are in balance. This journey of discovery showed me that outward peace is a reflection of inward truth. That inward truth only comes from one place—a strong, consistent relationship with Jesus Christ. When we pattern our way of coping with life's ruffles, we look to Him and His example. Jesus' ability to walk through chaos, replacing it with peace, stemmed from what was inside Him. He didn't allow any lies to take root and choke out God's truth. That foundational truth is that we cannot walk daily in peace when we're living inside a mess of rumpled—ruffled—feathers.

Feathering Your Nest

Ephesians 2:10 shows us how to live a daily unruffled life.

- First, as God's workmanship, we are formed with holy hands. In Genesis God pronounces His creation (us) good. Begin reforming how you see yourself by making a list of all the good qualities God has placed in you.

- Second. Consider the opportunities God has placed in your path. How has He worked through you to bless others?

Finally examine your daily walk. Are you allowing your circumstances to dictate your peace or are you drawing your attitude from the core of strength God has placed inside you? What are some ways you can live more fully from the inside out?

Birds of a Feather—Together
From Rhonda

I'm a little aggravated that some of the best counsel in this whole book comes from Edie's husband. Just kidding. I was, however, astonished by Kirk's words to his wife. "I think you need to figure out where this lie is coming from and how to get rid of it." He could've put together a persuasive argument about how beautiful Edie is, inside and out. Which she is. And he would've been right in doing that. But God gave him the wisdom to send his wife on a journey of sorting out lies and finding worth in the beautifully unruffling truth of God.

Dear Lord, make me a journey-sender, I pray.

Chapter Eight

When God Does the Ruffling

Rhonda

Oh that moment. That moment of extreme delight when the waiter brings out a spectacular tray covered with every dream dessert. *Be still, my heart.* Of course, for me, right after that moment of delight comes the next moment of complete despair when I realize the guy expects me to only take one.

Maybe that's one of the reasons I love cake pops. They're tiny. So that means you can eat a whole tray of them.

I also love cake pops because: Cake. On a stick. And apparently I now think even forks and plates are too much trouble.

I've wondered if dessert trays should come with instructions. Like, "choose only one." Or better: 1) Reconsider eating any of this. And then, 2) Never eat any of this.

I'm obviously still working on forming better habits. I'd like to eat less of this kind of stuff. Also I'd like to eat more of this kind of stuff. So that's where I am. More or less.

Habitually More, Habitually Less

It's a little similar in my faith life. Sometimes I long to see God do more. A new thing. Around me and in me and through me. To spread my unruffled feathers and fly like never before. When I pray and then stop and think what that might require, it pretty much always boils down to this: Less me. More Him.

There's no doubt I need to become much less satisfied with everything chocolate-covered and comfy-cozy and shift to a more resolute growing faith and join in the Kingdom work that will bring Him glory. More Spirit-directed intention. Less off-the-cuff, on-the-fly, and on-my-own.

I wonder how many miraculous happenings occur inside comfort zones. I'm thinking not many. Sometimes God brings us to a place outside our comfort, outside our strength, outside the box—sometimes maybe even outside of the possible. It's often in that place of squirming that He shows up biggest.

Between a Rock and a Thorny Place

No, I've not seen a lot of amazing moves of God born of comfort zones. But thorny places? That's a different story.

"A thorn in the flesh was given to me, a messenger of Satan to torment me so I would not exalt myself. Concerning this, I pleaded with the Lord three times to take it away from me. But He said to me, 'My grace is sufficient for you, for power is perfected in weakness.' Therefore, I will most gladly boast all the more about my weaknesses, so that Christ's power may reside in me. So I take pleasure in weaknesses, insults, catastrophes, persecutions, and in pressures, because of Christ. For when I am weak, then I am strong" (2 Corinthians 12:7-10 HCSB).

Want to see God do more? A new thing? In you, around you, and through you? Sometimes it happens in the thorniest places. It's accomplished in His strength and by His oh-so-sufficient grace. And here's the kicker. Whatever you can dream, He can deliver more. By His strength and grace, it's bigger. Better. More glorious.

Filled with Fullness, and Then Filling Some More

As Paul is telling the people in Ephesus about his desire that they be filled with "all the fullness of God" (Ephesians 3:19), he reminds them of the God who is "able to do above and beyond all that we ask or think according to the power that works in us" (vs. 20).

The Amplified Bible expands on verse 20 like this: "Now to Him who is able to carry out His purpose and do superabundantly more than all that we dare ask or think, infinitely beyond our greatest prayers, hopes, or dreams." More. And even more. And then superabundantly more!

Recognizing His "mores" will always result in the right kinds of "lesses." Less of my self-focused distractions. More of His glory. Less fretting about my comfort zone. More of the kind of service that will bring Him glory. It's the more and the less of living unruffled.

What Does That Mean for My Habits?

The habits might not always want to cooperate, by the way. For instance, in a more surfacey way, we've lived in the same house almost 15 years. That means I'm on about the 5,375th consecutive day of turning on the garbage disposal instead of the light. *Oi, that habit.*

I'm going to confess to you that while I was working on forming better habits, I thought I could start with a better breakfast routine. Surely I could at least pull together a bowl of cold cereal, right? But it was not as easy as you'd think. That first cardboard flap of a new cereal box? Major box-opening stress there. One wrong rip and the tab will never fit in the slot. You could hardly convince me I was not cutting diamonds.

Fast-forward to my discovery that I should never cut diamonds. The box looked like it had been opened by ferrets. Who probably don't even eat bran flakes. I wanted to quit—and that was before I got to the titanium-reinforced bag inside.

Seriously, what are those bags made of? While I'm asking questions, is bag-rage a thing? Because I may have had that. When you finally find the one weak spot in the forcefield of that bag, how many times does the cereal explode all over the kitchen?

People. If I was really meant to make this breakfast choice, wouldn't a box of cereal be easier to open than a bag of Oreos?

Make a Choice, Make a Difference

We make choices every day. Often, we can make a mess, make an excuse, make a scene, make a get-away—or make a difference. Sometimes we only get to pick one.

The fact is, good habits don't necessarily come with a switch to flick. We don't make good choices according to how easy they are.

They're built with perseverance. And I need to be reminded of this often. Peter obliges in 2 Peter 1:12-13. "Therefore I intend always to remind you of these qualities, though you know them and are established in the truth that you have. I think it right, as long as I am in this body, to stir you up by way of reminder." This kind of reminder is a worthy one to stir up the start of every new day. Another version communicates that stirring up this way: "to wake you up with a reminder" (HCSB). It's like waking up to a breakfast of champions, wouldn't you say?

In Doing the Due Diligence

I love looking at the verses right before that passage in 2 Peter in the Amplified version: "Therefore, believers, be all the more diligent to make certain about His calling and choosing you [be sure that your behavior reflects and confirms your relationship with God]; for by doing these things [actively developing these virtues], you will never stumble [in your spiritual growth and will live a life that leads others away from sin]" (2 Peter 10-11 AMP).

The "diligent" here is from the Greek "*spoudasate*," which means to labor over an endeavor—quickly and with earnestness. My natural selfishness prods me to choose garbage habits. The easy way. Flicking all the wrong switches.

Yet my God will give me the want-to to choose well, as we saw in chapter one, and then He will give me the ability to persevere in it. Paul said in Philippians 2:13, "For it is God who works in you, both to will and to work for his good pleasure."

Thinking Outside the Box-ing

Paul offers a great testimony in 1 Corinthians 9:26-27: "Therefore I do not run without a definite goal; I do not flail around like one beating the air [just shadow boxing]. But [like a boxer] I strictly discipline my body and make it my slave, so that, after I have preached [the gospel] to others, I myself will not somehow be disqualified [as unfit for service]" (AMP).

It's an entirely different kind of "boxing," I know. But I want to take on the challenge implied here with everything I've got. I want to make a difference.

Father, I have no doubt that You give me choices for a reason. You allow circumstances for a reason. I believe You often call me outside my comfort zone for a reason. Empower me, I pray, to choose well. To operate within Your reason. Work in me to accomplish Your good purpose for Your good pleasure. Out of my comfort zone, into Your will. I long to see You do something big in, around, and through me. Use my life—wrinkles, ruffles, and all—to make a difference in Your kingdom. Grant me the discipline to stay at it with perseverance, all for Your glory. Less me. More You. Let it be.

That's my prayer. And I so want to make a habit of praying it.

Feathering Your Nest

Longing to see God do more in you and through you? Are you ready to pray that prayer at the end of this chapter? Let me tell you, friend, at the point you pray it, hold on to your hat. I can tell you in the most personal way, He answers big prayers big. Big love, big mercy, big power, big grace. Look at the 2 Corinthians passage mentioned earlier in the Amplified version—the verses containing the Lord's response to Paul's thorn:

> "My grace is sufficient for you [My lovingkindness and My mercy are more than enough—always available—regardless of the situation]; for [My] power is being perfected [and is completed and shows itself most effectively] in [your] weakness" (2 Corinthians 12:9-10 AMP).

✒ Have you ever felt the Lord calling you out of your comfort zone? How did it ruffle your feathers? How did it grow your faith? How did it grow the Kingdom?

✒ "It's often in that place of squirming that He shows up biggest." Is there a holy nudge you've been sensing lately— one to step out in a big way? If so, what has been your response? And if you haven't felt a compulsion to step beyond your safe place recently, how can you plan to be prepped and ready when it comes?

- What big prayer will you pray today? When you pray it, zone in on His lovingkindness and mercy that are "more than enough—always available—regardless of the situation."

- Are you willing to make a habit of gracefully soaring in His calling? Willing and ready to habitually ask for "less me, more Him"? How does that habit make a person's life look different?

Birds of a Feather—Together
From Edie

Choices, more or less. I'm with Rhonda on this one—more chocolate, less bran. But seriously, I'm also in complete agreement—theoretically speaking—of more God and less me. Until I want something. Then the *me* inside seems to grow out of proportion to my good intentions. The tug of war begins and I want to win, but when I win I lose. So my resolve is now to lose—lose myself in the desires of Christ—and win the reward that satisfies even more than chocolate.

Change my desires to match Yours. Call me out of the comfort zone of what I want and into the unruffled flight of following You past new horizons.

Part Three:

Renewing a Ruffled Mind and Spirit

Most birds molt once a year. Losing its feathers leaves a bird looking messy and unkempt at best, and ugly and unhealthy at worst. Frequently feathers fall out in clumps and symmetrically so the bird is still aerodynamic enough for flight. Some, like water fowl, lose all their feathers at once and are unable to fly while the new growth takes place.

It's a difficult process, but one that's critical for the bird to stay healthy.

We can also experience a season of spiritual molting. God pulls out the old and unhealthy feathers and replaces them with new stronger quills. At times He even strands us in a certain place or time, forcing us to stay put as we wait for the new growth to take over and enable us to once again fly strong. Sometimes we may find ourselves in that difficult place of waiting for someone else's benefit. He never strands us alone, however. Or without reason. We can know because of the character and nature of our God that He never wastes a ruffle. Not one.

Chapter Nine

Accepting that Busyness is Not Bad

Edie

I have battled a distorted view of busyness my entire adult life. I started on one side of the spectrum and bounced to the other extreme before I settled into a place of peace and unruffled living.

At first I based my self-worth on how busy I was. The more items on my to-do list, the more my life had meaning. I lived a works-based philosophy. Following this mindset to its logical conclusion led me to believe that if activity made me more valuable then the contrary was true too. Inactivity—for whatever reason—meant my life had less value.

My Personal Struggle

When I was still a young mother—and a young believer—I also equated my busyness with being a good Christian. At church I served on committees, taught classes, and led ministries. At home I homeschooled our children, did my best to create a perfect home and be a supportive wife. All while answering God's call to write and speak.

From the outside I looked like super-woman. I worked hard to shore up that false persona. Inside I was crumbling, and the fragile belief system about who I was in Christ, began to turn to dust.

It disintegrated into a pile of rubble while my husband was half-way around the world on a business trip. That night, while my three young sons were upstairs asleep, I sat on the bathroom floor contemplating taking a bottle of pills and ending it all.

God gave me the strength to endure that endless night. Not from somewhere deep inside myself. Instead, He rallied His people. All night long, so regularly you could almost set a clock, my friends called me. Every hour the phone would ring and the conversation would begin the same way. "I'm so sorry to call, but God wouldn't leave me alone. Are you okay?"

Instead of acknowledging that I desperately needed help, I assured each one I was fine, but unable to sleep so the call was a comfort. Many of them still don't know how God used them to save my life that night.

The next day my husband arrived home, took one look at me and the bottles of pills still scattered around the bathroom and got me the help I so desperately needed.

My life changed radically, since the treatment plan subscribed by the doctors forced me stop everything I was doing. It was a dark time. I came face-to-face with what busyness-for-the-wrong-reason can do

Each activity I was forced to quit felt like an announcement of my failure. I stopped homeschooling and the boys were re-enrolled in public school—bad mother. I stopped all my teaching and serving at church—bad Christian. My house disintegrated into chaos, and we relied on the kindness of others to bring in meals— bad wife.

I expected my friends and acquaintances to drift away quietly, repulsed by my inadequacy. Instead, I seemed to gather more friends. Some called and chatted. Others dropped by for coffee. And many confessed that even though they hated what I was going through, they felt less intimidated by me. And God? He wrapped His arms around me, whispering love and hope into my soul without a trace of condemnation.

Not one person was disappointed by my inability to perform … not even God.

Slowly, through months of counseling and drug therapy, I rebuilt my life. My sons didn't perish from attending public school. My church didn't abandon me because I wasn't serving. My husband didn't hate me because I wasn't able to care for him and our children like a Pinterest mom. And God didn't rain down His wrath because I stopped *doing* for Him.

All my relationships blossomed with the sweetness of time and focus.

A Different Side of the Struggle

Then the pendulum swung, and I embraced the opposite extreme. In my mind, busyness was bad. My experience had taught me to believe that busy people were undisciplined and didn't know how to manage their lives. They couldn't choose the best, because they were rushing around doing all the good they could find to do.

I ran from busyness, shrinking away from opportunities God placed in my path. Deep inside I was terrified of returning the life that had brought me to my knees.

Now I know with certainty that neither mindset is valid or reasonable.

There are seasons of rest, seasons of busyness, and seasons of in-between times. That's the rhythm of life. But as our busyness quotient changes, we don't have to get our feathers in a ruffle. We can't measure our spirituality by the busyness of life.

Walking into a Season of Busyness with God

So what is my life now? I'm living in a season of busyness. No surprise that external chaos reigns considering the book I'm writing—and you're reading. I've noticed that whenever I begin to write a book, that is what God emphasizes in my life. I guarantee you that I'm learning far more from this book than you are.

Now busyness comes with a sweet peace and welling up of joy. It's definitely *not* because I'm some kind of super-spiritual believer. *(Rhonda, get off the floor and stop laughing.)* Instead peace and joy come from my heart. I'm no longer trying to prove my worth by activity and accomplishment. Now I'm responding to my close connection with God.

"The Lord directs the steps of the godly. He delights in every detail of their lives" (Psalm 37:23 NLT). I can feel God's presence as He walks with me through the fullness that's life right now. Working with Him deepens our connection and allows me to be more fully in His presence. I'm no longer the little girl saying notice me, like me, appreciate me. The desperate edge is gone as I enjoy a deep companionship with my heavenly father. Even though at times I'm busier than ever, I'm more often active with groomed feathers instead of ruffled ones.

Being a Christ-follower has its emphasis on the state of being verb, rather than an action verb. God has always been more interested in the process rather than the product. We must all remember that God is relationally—not task—oriented. Whatever needs doing, He can do. He uses us to accomplish His will not to keep us busy or because He Himself doesn't have the time. He allows us to join Him where He's working because of the relationship.

I've discovered that letting God set my priorities doesn't keep me from being drawn into the middle of chaos. Instead it allows me to walk through trying circumstances encased in a bubble of peace. My stress level goes through the roof when I'm trying to manage life in my strength. And that's the added benefit of letting God dictate the busyness quotient—when chaos reigns we're working in God's strength instead of our own.

This doesn't mean that God abandons us to our devices if we get into a self-made busy-storm. Far from it. I know because I'm still learning how to say yes to God and no to everything else. When I get over excited and make too much of my desires, all I have to do is to cry out to God, acknowledging my mistake, and He's right there to rescue me. God isn't waiting on me to ruffle my feathers and hit me with an "I told you so."

Putting it into Practice

So how do we focus on *being* rather than *doing* when a tornado of busyness blows our smooth feathers out of order?

I begin by praying over everything on my plate. I get specific with these prayers. I ask God for insight, the ability to perform under pressure, to relax into Him, and for Him to order my days, multiplying my time and covering all I do with joy.

Next, I check my mindset. This process means making certain that the busyness I'm experiencing comes from God instead from me saying yes apart from Him. I always go back to my one goal—my purpose is following God, not trying to prove I'm useful.

While praying and checking my mindset, I'm writing a priority list. Sometimes that list is driven by deadlines and dates, sometimes it's the urgency of what has to get done for other reasons. But I do it in tandem with prayer and review of my mindset because I never want to set my priorities apart from God's guidance.

Feathering Your Nest

As we work to apply this principle to our lives, let's look closer at Psalm 37:23, noting what is *doesn't* say as much as what it does tell us.

- The first part of this verse states that God directs the steps of the godly. This word *godly* implies those who are following Him. When we're walking in close proximity with God, we can discern His instruction much more clearly. What are some ways you can tell you are walking with God? How can you move even closer to Him?

- The second part of this verse reminds us that God delights in the details of our lives. He finds joy in us. Ask God to reveal some of the details about you that delight Him. Make a list and enjoy the fact that your heavenly Father finds delight your situation right now—even the tiniest parts.

- Now notice with me that there is no qualifier on this verse. It does *not* say this is only true when we get everything right and the busyness isn't our fault. As a matter of fact, the next verse gives us the assurance that God has made a provision for when we mess up. Read Psalm 37:24. Pull out your journal and record a time when God swooped in with abundant grace to keep you from falling when you made a mistake. When He rescues you, it's not an exception. God's delivery is part of the depth and breadth of His amazing love.

Birds of a Feather—Together
From Rhonda

How many times have we all based our worth and our spirituality on how busy we are? Or even how disciplined we are in avoiding that kind of chaos? I can't begin to express how I love and value my friend, Edie—and her transparency. I believe God honors that kind of humility, and even better, uses it to minister His grace. To me, to readers, to all those in Edie's sphere of influence. Her honesty causes me to cherish all the more this reminder of seasons of busyness, rest, and all the seasons between. I'm treasuring God's all-encompassing grace in every one of those seasons right now.

I praise You, my loving Father, for Your settling, buoying, inspiring, unruffling grace.

Chapter Ten

Squeeze the Day, Rein in the Worry-Ruffles

Rhonda

I know we've talked about an unruffled seizing of the day in this book. I wanted to make sure I included that I'm not always there. As a matter of fact, I'm often extremely not there.

There's no limit to what a person can accomplish … when that person is actually supposed to be diligently working on something else. For me, those moments of crazy-wild intensity somehow seem like the perfect times to go out and get my towels monogrammed or something. Maybe my luggage too.

Someone once told me that the sooner I fall behind, the more time I'll have to get caught up. That seemed logical. Personally, when I'm overwhelmed by a looming deadline or some other stressor, I try to be at least that logical.

For the record, I usually start well. First, I make a list. Then I put something on the list that I've already done so I can make at least one check mark on the list. Then I ignore the rest of the list and get on Facebook. I look at a handful of cat pictures, a scenic back porch or two, and several people's dinners. At that point I have to have a snack. Then I post a pic to all the social media sites of me eating my snack and make a great joke about how I'm snacking when I'm actually supposed to be working to meet that deadline.

I do remember that I'm supposed to seize the day. I really do. But sometimes the day is slippery.

Slip-Sliding Away

It's when a day is at its slipperiest I have to remember to shove aside the cute kitties, stop playing games on my iPad, and get a grip on what's important. Let me rush to say again in this book that living unruffled is not about not being busy. It's not. And it's certainly not always trying to squirm out from under a difficult schedule or task or problem. But we most definitely can aggravate ourselves and hinder our level of success in living well when we're not careful about how we spend our minutes.

I don't want to get to the end of life, look around at all I could've accomplished through Christ, and then be forced to comfort myself with something like, "Yeah, but look. I got the high score. And I've got this great luggage." I want to seize the day—every day. I want to start well and finish well.

And when I stop and think about it, I realize I don't want to merely seize the day. I want to get it in a headlock. I want to give it noogies until it cries like a little girl. I feel I'm having my best unruffled days when I've mercilessly wrestled out everything redeemable in the power of Christ. Squeezed it beautifully, fruitfully dry.

Not living in a lack of busyness or challenge or even trouble. But through it all, still fruitfully loving Jesus, fulfilling our calling, and still living in sweet closeness to the Father.

Start Well, Finish Well, Monogram Responsibly

That said, great unruffled-y benefits belong to those who are wise about how each minute is spent. Psalm 90:12 says, "Teach us to number our days carefully so that we may develop wisdom in our hearts" (HCSB). An "unnumbered" day is enveloped in foolishness. Life is too short for that. That's why I can't let myself get away with foolish carelessness. I must pay attention. "Pay careful attention, then, to how you walk—not as unwise people but as wise—making the most of the time, because the days are evil. So don't be foolish, but understand what the Lord's will is" (Ephesians 5:15-17 HCSB).

His will. That's where we start well. And it's there that we'll finish well. One Bible version expands on verse 16 and how to make the most of our time with "recognizing and taking advantage of each opportunity and using it with wisdom and diligence" (vs. 16, AMP). The best days are the ones in which I ignore everything slippery, and with wisdom and diligence, get the day in that headlock by breakfast, then have it whimpering before lunch.

So there's the challenge. Look the day straight in the eye, and then take it to the mat for the Kingdom. Make it cry a little. Some of us can dry the tears with monogrammed towels. But I worry that's not always a good thing.

Don't Worry Your Pretty Head

Speaking of worry. I have to wonder how much time I've worried away in my lifetime. I wonder how many times I've exchanged a wise and diligent squeeze of a day for a feathery fret. Could I have worried away a week? A month? Please tell me it's not years. *Ugh, what a thought.*

I'm not going to lie, I allowed my kids to make a few bad hair decisions as they were growing up, and I didn't worry about it. I worry a little *now* about the fact that it never worried me *then*. I did it for two reasons. 1) I knew I would be able to show them the pictures years later and tease them mercilessly, and 2) if everything was all hair perfection for them growing up, how would they ever learn to be funny?

May I say now, "well done, me." Because I have pictures. And the laughter is satisfying. And also, all my kids are hilarious.

I'm also big enough to admit that sometimes when we look at those pictures, the bad hair is mine. I'd rather call it a bad mousse day. Or as I've come to more often refer to it, "Serendipity-Do"— since I never knew exactly how that hair would turn out. Or how the gel would come off. When I say that I'm big enough to admit it, sometimes I mean my hair was big enough. Big enough for whatever. Oh my, the sheer bigness of that hair. I look at the photos of those three-story bangs and wonder how it all held up without girders and trusses. I think the highest hair stood with a lot of teasing, spraying, wishing and even more worrying. Plus another jar and a half of the gel-mousse-plaster-of-Paris of the day.

On a Wing and My Hair

Back then I also worried on windy days that those bangs might accidentally achieve enough thrust, drag, weight, lift and hairspray to fly me a couple of counties over. Oh the worries of heavy-duty aerodynamic bangs (hair-o-dynamic?). It's enough to … well … make your hair stand on end. Or turn it gray.

Worry in all aspects of life can be as sticky as cheap mousse. It's even sneaky. I often convince myself that worry is effective. After all, most of what worries me never happens. *Doesn't that mean it's working?*

Oh my, can we count the number of ruffles needless worry adds to a day?

Even in all its slick sneakiness, there's something we can do with worry. When we feel we're becoming ruffled and we're coming unglued (not a hair reference), and we don't know what to do, we have a choice. We can trade in that worry. "Do not be anxious or worried about anything, but in everything [every circumstance and situation], by prayer and petition with thanksgiving, continue to make your [specific] requests known to God" (Philippians 4:6 AMP).

Trading in the Worry-ruffles

Trading worry for prayer, petition, and thanksgiving? It's the most amazing trade. And you're not going to believe what comes along with it. A gloriously unexpected peace. That's right, an "unruffled-ness." We're told about it in the next verse. "And the peace of God [that peace which reassures the heart, that peace] which transcends all understanding, [that peach which] stands guard over your hearts and your minds in Christ Jesus [is yours]" (Philippians 4:7 AMP). Wow, a heart-and-mind-guarding peace straight from Jesus Himself. And it's ours!

Seeking Jesus—heart and mind wholly on Him—is the vital element. He said in Matthew 6:34, "So do not worry about tomorrow." He preceded that command with, "But first and most importantly seek (aim at, strive after) His kingdom and His righteousness [His way of doing and being right—the attitude and character of God" (Matthew 6:33 AMP). When His peace rules, the fears that seem three stories tall one minute, appear appropriately miniscule the next. Is there any worry—anything at all—that can stand up against the perfect peace of God?

God's peace has proven its ability to stand up against the biggest heartbreaks, the highest life-threats, or even the smallest and goofiest hair events—even events with pictures.

On the pics topic, I'm backing off my kids a hair. Possibly because for every shot I take at one of their styles, they can always pull out a Glamour Shot of mine (insert a sigh here—but not an altogether ruffled one).

Feathering Your Nest

We have enemies, friends. Satan is a shrewd enemy who would like nothing more than to trap us in ruffles and render us fruitless and frustrated. Our sin nature often wars against us too. Worry, distractions—all of it. We resist these enemies in faith and in casting.

> "Casting all your cares [all your anxieties, all your worries, and all your concerns, once and for all] on Him, for He cares about you [with deepest affection, and watches over you carefully]. Be sober [well balanced and self-disciplined], be alert and cautious at all times. That enemy of yours, the devil, prowls around like a roaring lion [fiercely hungry], seeking someone to devour. But resist him, be firm in your faith [against his attack—rooted, established, immovable], knowing that the same experiences of suffering are being experienced by your brothers and sisters throughout the world. [You do not suffer alone.] After you have suffered for a little while, the God of all grace [who imparts His blessing and favor], who called you to His eternal glory in Christ, will Himself complete,

confirm, strengthen, and establish you [making you what you ought to be]" (1 Peter 5:7-10 AMP).

🖋 What worry or distraction or wrong belief is getting in the way of you experiencing the unruffled life? Is there something holding you back from seizing every opportunity to live as you were created to live—in the fullness and freedom of a God who loves you "with deepest affection" and who "watches over you carefully"?

🖋 It's in our new nature to desire to see Christ "complete, confirm, strengthen, and establish" us—making us what we ought to be. Is there anything specific you would love to see the Father do in you? Ask Him to begin that work in you even now.

🖋 If worry is a hindrance, make a list of those worries that trouble you most. Is there anything on that list that's too hard for your God? Anything He can't handle? Cast those worries on Him in prayer, and let your thanksgiving to Him and praise for Him be the exclamation point to your prayer.

Birds of a Feather—Together
From Edie

I don't really know how Rhonda does it. She disarms us with her humorous humility and then ambushes us with arrows of spiritual truth. I was so glad she took the chapter on worry-ruffles because those are the most worrisome of all my ruffled situations. Her transparent thoughts bless us all as she reminds us to trade in worry-ruffles for prayer, petition, and thanksgiving. It's the kind of swap that makes even the most timid, worry-ridden soul relax. Next time worry takes center stage, I'm choosing Jesus over the uncomfortable ruffles worry brings.

The next time worry takes center stage, help me remember to choose Jesus over the uncomfortable ruffles worry brings.

Chapter *Eleven*

Hiding Under God's Wings

Edie

He will cover you with His feathers; you will take refuge under His wings. His faithfulness will be a protective shield" (Psalm 91:4 HCSB).

Sometimes the unruffled feathers we need belong to God.

I love the visual of this verse—probably because I've experienced the truth pictured here many times. There are places in life that go far beyond ruffled feathers. Situations that make us feel plucked and ready for the stewpot. When those *I-can't-fix-this* moments descend, and the peace inside is gone, we still have a place to go.

When Life Unravels

I vividly recall one of those moments several years ago, when my world came crashing down in an instant. Our youngest son was playing in a baseball tournament, and my husband got up to get our jackets from the car. Seconds later, we found him lying face down on the asphalt parking lot

As I rushed to Kirk's side, my mind raced ahead for possible scenarios—heart attack, stroke, hit and run? I knelt beside him and rolled him on his back. Blood poured from his obviously broken nose as others came to our aid. Someone called 911 and my husband swam to consciousness, confused and incoherent.

He couldn't tell us what happened and all we could do was keep him still and wait for the ambulance. To me it seemed like hours before help arrived. Later I learned it took less than three minutes. It was during that stretch of time, as I continued to cry out to God to fix this, that His peace descended.

The EMTs arrived, checked my husband's heart, stabilized his neck with a collar, and loaded him into the ambulance. There were numerous offers to drive me to the hospital, but I declined and followed the flashing lights alone, using the time to pray out loud and prepare for what might come.

At the hospital, chaos reigned. But for me, calm assurance was my covering. I felt I was viewing the situation from beneath the protection of God's perfect peace. I had scurried into my heavenly Father's unruffled presence and could function as needed.

Tests were done and still there was no obvious reason for my husband's loss of consciousness. But finding the why was secondary to treating the resulting injuries. In the hours that passed I learned those injuries were devastating. Kirk had shattered every bone in his face, broken his jaw in three places, and possibly sustained serious injury to his spine. It took two hours and two radiologists to determine he hadn't broken his neck. For his face, they called in a specialist in facial reconstructive surgery. My two older sons arrived at the hospital, staying with Kirk while I met with the doctor.

The doctor led me to a consultation room to explain the extent of his injuries and reveal the plan of care. But it was the first words he spoke that proved God was in control. "God is the Creator and He does the best job, but with His help, we're going to put your husband back together, and he will be fine." This doctor was a top specialist in his field; he was also a believer.

They finally determined the cause of the accident—an extreme drop in blood pressure. Although the next few months were tough, God worked daily miracles and life eventually returned to normal.

I would never be the same.

Moving On

Although I'd experienced God's presence and His unexplainable peace before, I'd never operated *from* that covering for such a long time. It was like living in the eye of a hurricane—with full power and working Internet. At first those close to me thought I was in shock and they hovered close, waiting for reality to settle and me to fall apart. It never happened. Let me be clear, it was *not* because I was strong—emotionally or spiritually. The miracle of how I coped was one hundred percent because God had me safely tucked beneath His wings.

So why do we wait for the desperate situations before we allow God to be the peace we need? For years before my husband's accident, I'd overlooked this obvious source of comfort and strength. I moped around, feathers more bedraggled than ruffled, determined to be strong enough to handle whatever life shoved my way. Sometimes other, less drastic situations, push us into potholes of spiritual exhaustion. Turns out God loves for us to run beneath His sheltering wings for the little problems as well as the big ones.

It wasn't too long past the chaos of my husband's accident when I had the chance to test what I'd learned. I was dealing with a difficult professional relationship, and my feelings had been hurt when I was accused, judged, and condemned by someone I trusted. My emotions were erratic. I needed to forgive and move on, but I also thought I needed some kind of closure. So I began obsessing. I envisioned scenario after scenario where I would have the opportunity to communicate to this person my view of what had occurred.

There was nothing life-threatening or even life-damaging about the circumstances, but I couldn't let it go. My feathers wouldn't stop ruffling. Finally, during an honest quiet time, I poured out everything I was feeling to God. The sensation that followed was one of being swept close to his body and covered by His wings. He blocked the hurt and the obsessive thoughts and gave me a place to rest. I snuggled close to His heart while my ragged emotions began to heal. In the days that followed, every time my emotions began to overwhelm, I rushed back to that safe place and let Him protect me from the situation.

Living From God's Covering
All this makes enjoyable reading—we hope. But that's not the point to this book. We know how important it is to be able to

translate concepts into specific steps we can take to apply them to our lives.

I try to organize my life to point to God and help me remember to apply the truth God has taught me. I hate having to learn the same lesson again and again. So I decorate my life with visual reminders. I've found that I'm easily distracted—especially when my feathers are in a fluff, and sometimes it takes a physical reminder to redirect me out of the kerfuffle and into God's presence.

I have Bible verses written on scraps of paper and taped in places I frequent. Psalm 91:4 is above my desk. I have decor that points me to God—lots of birds and feathers at my house. I also have a collection of mercury glass. Random, I know. But for me this beautiful old glass carries a visual meaning.

Its reflective quality helps me remember to reflect God in all circumstances.

The weathered, imperfect nature of the glass reminds me that I don't have to be perfect to shine or have beauty.

Finally, almost all the mercury glass pieces I own are vessels— on purpose—that's another nudge to remember that I'm at my best when I'm empty of myself and full of God.

All of these visual cues are preparation for the chaotic storms that life inevitably throws at us. Beyond this, a group of special women are accountability and prayer partners. I'd like to take the credit for hand-picking these women, but God put us all together.

Finally—and most importantly—I spend time on my relationship with God. I make Him a priority. I don't squeeze Him into the moments between chaos, or ignore Him until I need Him. I start the day with Him, and I end it with Him. Yes, during seasons of insanity, that time may be brief, but it's still there. Spending this time with Him ensures that I recognize His voice when He speaks to me—even in the midst of a howling gale.

Feathering Your Nest

As you get further acquainted with the safe place under God's wings, let's explore the concept more closely.

- In Psalm 91:4, notice that the verbs are present tense and emphatic. He *will* cover you, you *will* take refuge, His faithfulness *will*. This verb isn't a wish, it's a certainty. Consider what "will" means in your current circumstances. How does this present tense verb renew your hope and bring peace?

- Consider ways you can be quicker to run to God's covering when ruffles occur. What steps can you take now to prepare for the storms to come?

- Assemble your accountability/prayer team. The women I meet with regularly aren't there only for me—we're there for each other. Ask God to help you begin a group if you don't already have one. If you are blessed with a group, ask Him to show you how to strengthen it.

Birds of a Feather—Together
From Rhonda

Hiding under our God's protective wing. I love this. And I so appreciate that His love and grace and protection are not reserved only for the enormously traumatic events, but for every event. I've heard it said that often our biggest challenges are not so much in the huge crises. We usually run to God first for those, because we recognize they're too big for us to handle. But the challenge often lies in the broken shoelaces—in the day-to-day frustrations that we figure we can take care of on our own. Thank you, Edie, for this reminder.

And thank You, Lord, for Your love, Your care, Your safe place, Your wing.

Chapter Twelve

How to Take Heart, Not Lose Heart

Rhonda

My family. We're all pretty much a big bunch of losers. No, not like that. I mean more like: "Hey, have you seen my phone?" "Guys, where in the world are my keys?" "Anybody got an extra pen because I can't find mine?" "Do you see my glasses anywhere in here?" "Wasn't I wearing a coat when I came in?"

We're forever setting something down and walking off like we're never going to need it again. Here's a favorite one of mine: "This is a big parking lot, I was only in the store for 15 minutes, and yet I have for sure and forever lost my car." I don't think there's even a string I could tie around a finger to help remind me where I put that.

In a "how much can one family lose" contest, ironically, we would win. My entire family. Losers.

Losin' It

I might also lose my mind, lose my nerve, lose my way, lose my grip, lose my edge, or maybe even lose my cool. But there is one thing I never want to lose. I never want to lose heart.

"Hey, have you guys seen my heart? Where in the world did I leave that thing?"

To lose heart is to seriously ruffle. It's to lose the joy we find in knowing we are victors in Jesus. At a loss of heart, we start to wimp out in the walk of faith and toy with the idea of quitting the pursuits that count. *Hello, life of ruffles.* I don't have to find my glasses to see this: my heart is never off track when every part of it is laser-focused on Christ. We're told to consider Him in just that way in Hebrews 12:3: "For consider him who endured such hostility from sinners against himself, so that you won't grow weary and give up," (CSB).

Consider Him. Think about Him. Realize who He is. Credit Him for what He's done. When we do, we are miraculously heartened. "Give up" in the Hebrews verse reads as "lose heart" in several translations. It's from a Greek term that means to untie. To be unstrung. It's to be overcome by circumstances. Altogether ruffled. Considering our God—that's it. That's how we "take" heart instead of losing it. Psalm 69:32 says, "You who seek God, take heart!" (CSB), and then a few verses earlier, we're reminded of one great way to find the ability to do it, "I will praise God's name with song and exalt him with thanksgiving" (Psalm 69:30).

Consider This

Worship, thanksgiving, and praise are a little like a string we tie around our heart to help us remember. Thanksgiving is not a one-time, seasonal excuse for a turkey dinner. We don't pull it out once a year, then set back down and walk away from it like we're never going to need it again. Thanksgiving and praise and worship of our God are the natural result of "considering Him." Truly considering Him so that we don't lose heart, we don't give up, we're not unstrung, we remain unruffled.

I may lose my keys—often—but I want to hang on to this truth. I want to stay ever aware of my wonderful God. I want to ask Him often and sincerely to show me how to worship well, and to guard my heart, never letting me set it down, never forgetting what matters most. Never focusing on worthless things. That beautiful place of "unruffled" heartens my heart in worship, thanksgiving, and praise.

I may forget many people and many places. But not that place of intimacy with Him.

More Musing on Losing

And not that it's anywhere nearly as important to remember as that place is, but on a different level, it is still at least somewhat important to me to remember: the coffee.

I microwaved my second cup of coffee a few mornings ago and couldn't figure out why in the world it tasted like cough medicine. Granted, I'm never sure how I'm supposed to be awake enough to get my coffee when I've yet to have my coffee.

Three or four sips in, I still didn't get why it tasted so weird. Somewhere around that fifth sip, I woke up enough to remember it wasn't my second cup of coffee. It was my first. And then another realization slowly started to sink in: *I haven't made the coffee yet this morning.*

I stared at that cup of coffee for several minutes thinking about how I've been gone for a few days and *Oh my word. When* did *I make this coffee?*

Let's be clear. There are times when adding extra creamer isn't going to cut it. Not even a lot of creamer. Not even if it's caramel macchiato creamer. Cough-medicine-au-lait is never going to be anybody's specialty drink of the day. And frankly, I'm pretty sure those first four sips were a little chewy. No wait. I think I'll stay in denial about that for a while longer.

Coffee? Or Cough-ee?

It's a good reminder, though, that sin can be something like that.

Worshipping the Lord, taking heart, is a step into the light that can expose dark places in our hearts. When we encounter His holiness, we become painfully aware of our unholiness apart from the borrowed righteousness of Christ. At those worship encounters, we need to take note that we don't make life taste better by trying to flavor sin with something we think might mask its icky-ness. We don't fix anything by excusing or rationalizing. Denial doesn't work. We can't avoid dealing with its objectionableness by distracting ourselves with something else or otherwise trying to forget about it either. What we have to do every time is just plain get rid of it.

Pour it out. Get a clean cup. Start over. We confess sin, turn away from it, and go a different direction.

Facing up to our sin is anything but tasty. It's unpleasant. Humiliating, even. But necessary. Refusing to confront and deal with sin leads us on a downward spiral to Ruffle Town. At every point we come face to face with our sin, we get a closer look at our depravity and our surprising penchant for evil. It's easy to deceive ourselves about our bent to sin, but this is no place for denial. Just one taste of our sin's offensiveness, the revelation that we could actually be so utterly wicked, can be outright devastating. It sends us into a place of mourning.

Oh What a Beautiful Mourning

But it's at that place of mourning that Jesus comes alongside us. When we become agonizingly aware of our inability to lift the tiniest finger to clean up the mess, and at the point we realize anew our complete dependence on Him to do it, He reminds us of His cross. His payment for every sin was complete. Jesus suffered unspeakable agony on that cross for sin—agony that should've been ours.

Remembering the inexpressibly high price of sin also reminds us to keep a short account of it. First John 1:9 reminds us that "If we confess our sins, he is faithful and just to forgive us our sins and to cleanse us from all unrighteousness." Not a masking. Not a distraction. Not a denial. No, a complete cleansing. A new cup, as it were. That's a better something to chew on every morning. One of the best ways to take heart is to make sure that heart is clean—and that's all because of Christ.

In other things to remember, making sure I've put on a new pot of coffee is higher up there on my to-do list every morning. I'm happy to report that at least that morning of ick coffee didn't make me sick. As a matter of fact, I don't think I coughed once the entire day.

Feathering Your Nest

What could be sadder than losing heart? What could be more life-ruffling? Keeping a short account of sin is vital in living in an unruffled faith. We read David's charge to take heart.

> "Be strong and take heart, all you who hope in the Lord" (Psalm 31:24 NIV).

> "Blessed is the one whose transgressions are forgiven, whose sins are covered. Blessed is the one whose sin the Lord does not count against them and in whose spirit is no deceit. When I kept silent, my bones wasted away through my groaning all day long. For day and night your hand was heavy on me; my strength was sapped as in the heat of summer. Then I acknowledged my sin to you and did not cover up my iniquity. I said, 'I will confess my transgressions to the Lord.' And you forgave the guilt of my sin" (Psalm 32:1-5 NIV).

From this psalm, jot down a list of every ruffly feeling David had when he was ignoring, denying, or covering up his sin. Some consequences were spiritual and emotional. Some were physical. Have you ever held off confessing sin to the Lord and experienced that kind of fallout?

Contrast and compare the two kinds of "covering" for sin in the passage.

Is there any sin you've been holding on to? Are you ready to let go of what's holding you back, take heart again, and soar in unruffled, victorious forgiveness? Whether or not you have a sin issue you're dealing with, ask the Lord to help you keep a short sin account. Thank Him for His faithful reminders to do just that.

Birds of a Feather—Together
From Edie

Tying a string around my heart—that's a word picture I can sink my teeth into. The idea of using worship, thanksgiving, and praise as a way to not lose heart is more than genius, it's truth—Jesus truth. Battling ruffled feathers is an ongoing fight, but when we let Jesus do the heavy lifting, we're always on the winning side.

Don't let me forget that You are always present and more than able.

Part Four:

Grabbing onto Peace in a Ruffled World

Feathers don't merely benefit one single bird. They also provide an important part in nest building, caring for eggs, and nurturing chicks. Especially in desert climates, feathers play an important role in transporting water.

Often adult birds will soak the feathers on their bellies in water before returning to the nest. This keeps the eggs from drying out and once the chicks have hatched, provides them with much needed water.

Some birds, like the sandgrouse, have feathers that are specifically designed to hold water. This allows them to nest further from watering holes and keeps them safer from predators.

God also provides the renewing water of His Spirit and His Word when we accept it. As He hides us beneath the cover of His wings, He not only gives us much-needed protection, but a cool refreshing drink from the well that never goes dry. By His very presence, He will comfort, satisfy, and quench us through every difficult, ruffling challenge.

Chapter *Thirteen*

Attitude Affects Altitude—A Grateful Heart Smooths our Feathers

Edie

Sce, I am doing a new thing! Now it springs up; do you not perceive it? I am making a way in the wilderness and streams in the wasteland" (Isaiah 43:19 NIV).

This Bible verse is a perky sort when it comes to change—and one that took me a long time to embrace. I'm not a big fan of modification. Many of my friends and family would agree that I am change challenged. I see change in a negative light. Get me out of my routine—any routine—and my feathers begin to ruffle. My first response to a new way of doing any part of life is to grumble and complain, bringing me spiraling into a crash landing.

I can't seem to help it. Any time the unexpected happens I immediately jump to the whinier side of what-if. However, God has worked hard to teach me that within every calamity, every stress, every bump in the road, there is the potential for blessings. And a place for counting those blessings. Because gratitude smooths so many ruffly situations.

I've found that attitude affects altitude. It's hard to fly with wings full of ruffled—negative—feathers. It's also almost impossible to focus on the blessings of God and be miserable. Being grateful sets us free to soar, seeing the circumstances of life through God's eyes. While being negative shifts the focus downward and limits us to seeing only the problem.

A Shift in How I Viewed Change

There was a time when I was anything but grateful with the life I'd been given. When our oldest child was still an only child, my husband's job forced us to move frequently—about every four to six months. These weren't minor moves either. Most were across several state lines. About eighteen months into this vagabond lifestyle, I was over the adventure and feeling frustrated. Inside resentment about the fact that I could never put down roots began to bubble and boil.

It takes time to settle into a community, find a church, friends, and a mother's morning out program for kids. Even though I could acclimate to a new city with lightning speed, these connections couldn't be rushed. So about the time I had begun to settle in, it was time to move again. But after one incident my perspective changed.

My husband announced that we'd be moving again—in less than a week. Tears burned my eyes, and a lump in my throat kept me from speaking. We'd found a church, and I'd been invited to hang out with a few of the ladies there. Now I'd be packing to leave instead of developing new friends.

I was lonely and desperately tired of always being the new person in town. I wanted friends and a more permanent place to call home.

During supper my husband shared where we'd be heading, when we'd be leaving, and all the details he'd learned about the new area. But I couldn't work up any excitement. I felt exhausted by the process.

After we tucked our son into bed, my husband tried to get me to talk about my misgivings. As the complaints tumbled out, he nodded and listened. The he proposed a deal.

"Instead of looking at these moves as an opportunity to put down deep roots, let's look at them as long vacation spots."

Those words stopped me in my tracks. A new perspective. And since our destination this time was the Atlantic coast of Florida, the idea had possibilities.

He continued, "I'm not saying we shouldn't find a church or make friends. We'll do that. But let's also take advantage of living in all these cool places. Let's be tourists who have *time* to explore."

That's exactly what we did. This shift in thinking changed my entire perspective. Once again I was able to get excited about the adventure. We were there for six months and had a marvelous time visiting all the interesting spots nearby.

Applying the Lesson I Learned

That experience impacted the way I look at life, and it taught me that my gratitude quotient was directly tied to my attitude. Now, when my feathers get ruffled because of the latest challenge to my routine, I look for reasons to be grateful. It's been a process, learning how to react unruffled when inside every feather is standing straight up.

One practice has helped keep my gratitude on the positive side and negative outlook … well … in the negative, has the been keeping a gratitude journal. Writing has always been one of the ways I process life. Listing my blessings on a daily basis brings a whole new dimension to my attitude.

If you've never kept a gratitude journal, I recommend giving it a try. I love beautiful notebooks and fancy pens, but if you have a more minimalist style, you can easily record your blessings in the notes section of your phone. It's important to write them somewhere. For me, simply listing them in my mind isn't enough. I have too many random thoughts in my brain to try to keep up with a list.

It's easy to get in a rut with gratitude journaling. So I have some guidelines I follow.

- I keep a gratitude journal on a monthly calendar, trying to keep the blessings list current. In other words, I don't write about last week's blessings, I find something I'm grateful for on that specific day.

- I record only three or four on each day

- I never repeat anything within that month.

- If I run into a problem finding something to be grateful for, I use the G. L. A. D. method of gratitude journaling to remind me.

1. **G** reminds me to remember something I'm *grateful* for.
2. **L** reminds me to consider a lesson I've *learned.*
3. **A** reminds me to recognize a goal I've *accomplished.*
4. **D** reminds me to recall what *delighted* me.

My memory is always refreshed with the GLAD method.

By teaching myself to look for the blessings in every situation, I've been able to soothe my ruffles and even avoid a few.

Feathering Your Nest

I believe there is a purpose for everything in our lives. The good, the bad, and even the ugly have been sifted by God to bring something good. I'm not saying everything that happens is good. We live in a messed-up world. But God is so much bigger. He takes the imperfections and tragedies of this world and brings good out of them. It's hard to see God in some instances, but He's there, if we only look for Him.

How has being grateful and recognizing a blessing helped you to change your attitude and ruffles?

Consider a difficulty you're facing right now—it can be big or small. Say a prayer, asking God to show you how to find the good in it. Then share what you discover.

Isaiah 43:19 tells us God is "making a way in the wilderness and streams in the wasteland." How does gratitude help us cut through the junk in our lives and bring refreshing to our souls?

Birds of a Feather—Together
From Rhonda

I wonder how many times I've flapped and fluttered in the biggest ruffle, only to discover that the ruffle does not define my life. Or me. There's much more to this existence than that one negative. That big, fluffy negative, however, tends to have a lot louder presence when I allow it. I have so much to be grateful for all around and about my negative ruffle. And I dare say, I can even be thankful for that ruffle—and how God can use it in positive ways. Before I know it, making myself at home in a place of gratitude has me saying, "Well hello, attitude adjustment!"

Thank You, even now, for how You are using every ruffle.

Chapter *Fourteen*

Peace-shaping Focus

Rhonda

It takes focus to meet a deadline. And yet, this morning? My testimony:

Me: Hey self, you really should be working on those four crazy-pressing, freaky-close, time-to-panic deadlines.

My brain: Yeah but how 'bout we put up a weird status on Facebook and have a snack instead?

Me: Okay well I guess you know best.

So yes, it's true that focus is not my best feature. I found a piece of bread in the toaster this morning. I put it in there yesterday. At least I hope it was yesterday. Now that I think about it, that almost-toast looked like the raisin bread I never bought. Focus is not my best feature and also toast is not my best feature. I couldn't even focus long enough to press down a lever.

Toastifying, Peace Supplying

Our focus can determine so much about a day. As I can obviously testify. If not toastify. Constantly focusing on negatives, for instance, leaves us burned out and ruffled up in the worst ways—completely over-toasted. Fixing our thoughts and focus on what we don't have or can't do, focusing on our failures and fears, or focusing on every difficulty in a day can leave us feeling overwhelmed and undone.

Yet what happens as we focus on our all-powerful, all-knowing, magnificently merciful, and loving God? It's almost surprising how instantly peace pops up.

Not only peace. More like double peace. Isaiah 26:3-4 says, "You keep him in perfect peace whose mind is stayed on you, because he trusts in you. Trust in the Lord forever, for the Lord God is an everlasting rock."

The "perfect peace" is described here in the Hebrew as "peace, peace." Both sides. Every side, actually. Fully cooked. Nothing lacking.

This Is Only a Test

Want to know how to test your focus? Take a look at the peace you're experiencing. Or *not* experiencing. The passage in Isaiah promises the Father's perfect double-peace for the mind that is "stayed" on Him—dependent. It's a mind so focused that thoughts of this trustworthy God are the brain's default.

Our natural default apart from Christ is self-focus. The more we focus on self, the more ruffled, stressed out, and dissatisfied we are with life. As a matter of fact, focusing on self will take us further away from what we're meant to be.

Yet placing our life-focus on the Lord brings peace into our lives even in difficult, stressful, or four-deadline circumstances. They can't toast our peace when our minds are truly focused on the trustworthy God who is our peace.

We are often shaped by our focus. If we concentrate on the negative or tests or just our selfish selves, that's the shape our character and life will take on. The more we focus on the Lord and His truths, the more His Spirit shapes us to look like *Him.* He can even shape life to look exactly like perfect double-peace.

Double Whammy

Back when I had to take all five of my kids shopping, I remember thinking I needed to double up on the peace. There always seemed to be some challenge threatening to ruffle me on every level. Not only did I have to try to check off all the items on my shopping list, but I had to try to keep any and all other merchandise undamaged and in its original spot.

Sometimes when you're trying to keep five kids together in a grocery store, it feels like trying to coral baby hummingbirds. Plus, I had to leave the store with the same number of hummingbirds I came in with. Preferably all the exact same ones I came in with.

Shopping excursions. They were not short on suspense, intrigue, drama—humming. I wonder if any of them would've made a good movie. I did consider hiring a cellist at one point to follow us around playing ominous music.

Stringing Them Along, Heavy on the Strings

When those five littles were all so young, it felt like a win anytime we made it to the checkout with no one bawling. Joy! As in, change that cello tune to a lively piece of Bach's, thank you very much.

There were a few times when I did the "we're still happy and it's checkout time" dance, only to get behind that person who seemed compelled to hunt for one specific coupon for 18 minutes. While I corralled hummingbirds. Increase drama. Increase cello volume, slow the tempo.

The cello. What a versatile instrument. And mysterious. Doesn't it seem to communicate gloom or ecstasy and everything in between at the turn of a music page and a tug on a bow?

Joice and Re-Joice

Keeping up the lively beat of joy in our faith walk can seem mysterious too. In Philippians 4:4, Paul commands, "Rejoice in the Lord always." And if that's not clear enough, he repeats that refrain: "again I will say, rejoice." It's like he's saying, "never *don't* rejoice." The book of Philippians addresses some anything-but-lively thoughts. Paul talks about the possibility of being put to death for his faith even. And yet, there it is: rejoice. Always.

How can we always rejoice? Sometimes life is hard, and sometimes we feel deep sadness.

Rejoice is a verb. To rejoice is to set joy into motion. There's a power behind it. And the power doesn't kick in until we realize it's not ours. Paul gives us the forward motion in the Philippians 4:4 command. He does it in three words: "in the Lord." Too often we get hung up on the "always" and forget that it's only found "in the Lord." Joy is part of the fruit of the Spirit, and the Holy Spirit of God is not indwelling you part-time. He indwells you always. So He enables your joy *always.*

I love how our peace and our joy are so beautifully tied together. In and by the Spirit of God. "But the fruit of the Spirit is love, joy, peace, patience, kindness, goodness, faithfulness, gentleness, and self-control... If we live by the Spirit, let us also keep in step with the Spirit" (Galatians 5:22-25).

"Keep in step with the Spirit"—that's like music to our ears. To our lives! So yes, let's move forward in peace and joy in the power of the One who fills our hearts with singing, no matter what's going on around us.

Voila! Or Viola—Whichever Has Strings

Tap your toe. "Keep in step with the Spirit." Measure-by-measure, note-by-note, and voila! You can find yourself singing that joyful tune.

By the way, that's "voila" not "viola." Because here? No strings attached.

Feathering Your Nest

Let's take a closer look at the fruit of the Spirit in the Amplified version of the Bible:

> "But the fruit of the Spirit [the result of His presence within us] is love [unselfish concern for others], joy, [inner] peace, patience [not the ability to wait, but how we act while waiting], kindness, goodness, faithfulness, gentleness, self-control. Against such things there is no law. And those who belong to Christ Jesus have crucified the sinful nature together with its passions and appetites. If we [claim to] live by the [Holy] Spirit, we must

also walk by the Spirit [with personal integrity, godly character, and moral courage—our conduct empowered by the Holy Spirit]" (Galatians 5:22-25 AMP).

Peace and joy are right there for the asking. Will you ask, noting the amazing weightiness of those last five words, "empowered by the Holy Spirit?"

This joy and peace can be beautifully packaged in a bundle kind of deal, all empowered by the same Spirit. Is there one particular joy or peace in that package you feel you're experiencing less than the other? If so, this is a great opportunity to examine your life focus. Is it the kind of focus that inspires an unruffled life full of peace and joy? If not, what can you do to get there?

Here's one more joy verse to meditate on, straight from Jesus. He said, "These things I have spoken to you, that my joy may be in you, and that your joy may be full" (John 15:11). And another peace verse that Edie mentioned earlier bears meditation. These are the words of our Savior as well. "I have said these things to you, that in me you may have peace. In the world you will have tribulation. But take heart; I have overcome the world" (John 16:33). Spend some time thanking and praising the Lord of peace and joy.

Birds of a Feather—Together
From Edie

Focus. A topic so dear to this photographer-gal's heart. I get the need, but sometimes the subject I choose isn't quite right. In this chapter Rhonda shares the necessity of staying intent on the One that brings everything into perspective—Jesus focus. So how do we stay laser-locked on Jesus? By stringing together joy and peace. I love how Rhonda reminds us that rejoice is the verb that sets joy in motion. And moving in joy unruffles our feathers as we soar to new heights, and along the way, experiencing the peace that only Jesus gives.

Give me Your peace and the ability to live in active joy!

Chapter *Fifteen*

Know Your Feathers

Edie

Prayer plays an important part of living in unruffled peace. In spite of the fact that I've written numerous books on prayer, the act of praying didn't always come easy to me. It bothered me that prayer didn't come easy. I felt like it was a black mark against me that I couldn't be comfortable praying. I managed to ignore it and avoid prayer until I began having children. Then, the urgency to have a strong prayer life hit with a vengeance, and my prayer life became vitally important. I wanted to be the type of mom who prayed powerful prayers that protected her children no matter what happened.

Three active sons was—and still is—enough to make my feathers stand on end! Even now they're grown, they keep me on my knees.

A Mother's Nightmare

There was one instance several years ago that reminded me of the importance of prayer for those we love. Two of my sons planned a day trip kayaking in the northern part of our county. Both of them are experienced outdoorsmen, so it shouldn't have been cause for concern. But it was summer, and we were experiencing the typical August pop-up severe thunderstorms. Lightning and water don't mix, it doesn't matter how experienced the kayaker.

Even though the morning was clear and the weather perfect, I felt a momentary catch in my heart when they got ready to pull out of the driveway. *What if a thunderstorm came up suddenly?* I wanted to warn them to be careful and pay attention, or better yet, stay home. I knew it would be pointless. They'd roll their eyes and shake their heads at their silly old mother. So instead of voicing my fears, I told them to have fun and took my motherly worries to the One who could ensure safety. It wasn't a pretty prayer, but it was heartfelt, and I repeated it several times that afternoon. My prayer brought me peace and although I didn't hear from them that evening, I felt an assurance that they were fine.

The next day I found out just how close I'd come to losing both sons.

Ruffled Waters

Sure enough a strong storm blew in on top of them. They'd paddled toward shore, but never made it. Three-and-a-half hours later they awoke, each one alone and disoriented. One was caught by his life jacket on a snag in the middle of the river, the other was laying half in and half out of the water on the shore. Neither one of them had his boat or any of his gear. It took them about ten minutes to locate one another and both confessed to me just how horrible that ten minutes had been. They had sustained some significant injuries—burns, severe headaches, nausea, and dizziness. As they catalogued the damage they concluded they'd been struck by lightning.

Thankfully they're both fine and carried no lasting affects away from the experience. I, on the other hand, still cringe mentally when I think about what could have happened. It's made me much more diligent to pray for my kids—no matter how old they are.

Raising offspring like these, I frequently found my feathers in a knot over whether or not my prayers were good enough. I evaluated my prayers, trying to decide if I'd spent enough time on thanksgiving or confession. What if I had the different parts of prayer out of order? In all my desire to become a good pray-er, I was looking for a formula. I wanted the perfect blueprint that would infuse my prayers with power enough to get God's undivided attention. And trying to wing it without a prayer map was getting my feathers all in a ruffle!

Knowing My Role

Turns out that what I believed about my role in prayer was backward.

I was looking for power in my words and in the presentation, instead of focusing on the power of God. I had forgotten that we have God's undivided attention—always. He loves each of us with a depth that defies description.

Even when I discovered the mistake in my thinking about prayer, I still wasn't quite sure how to frame my prayers. Then I reread a familiar passage in the Bible with new understanding. "So will My Word be which goes forth from My mouth; It will not return to Me empty, Without accomplishing what I desire, And without succeeding in the matter for which I sent it" (Isaiah 55:11 NASB).

This new perspective on talking to God was what I needed to get my prayer life on the right track. I began praying God's Word back to Him, and doing so revolutionized my prayer life, giving me a new confidence in so many ways.

First, by basing my prayers on His Word, I had the unruffled assurance I was praying in God's will. I didn't have to second guess how to pray or the words to use.

This kind of prayer also gave me a greater familiarity with God's Word. When you're using the Word for prayer, your understanding of Scripture deepens.

Finally, by relying on His words, I was relinquishing the responsibility of being good enough at prayer and acknowledging that prayer starts and ends with God.

Armed with this new assurance, I have deepened my prayer life using these three simple steps.

- I began praying specific verses during my prayer time. If I was praying for someone, I'd insert his or her name in place of any pronouns.

- I started a prayer journal. For me, it was too easy to get lost in prayer. Once I began writing out my prayers, I found it was possible to stay focused.

- I recorded how God spoke and how He moved. Often as I was praying, I would feel God directing my prayers and/or adding to them. By recording these insights from God, I could go back later and see how He had worked. I also went back later and added in how God answered these prayers.

These three simple steps revitalized my prayer life. By taking the focus off me and putting it back on God, the peace returned. With that peace, my faith also took wings and began to grow.

Feathering Your Nest

Prayer is non-negotiable in the life of a believer. But the power behind those prayers isn't our responsibility. Our part is obedience, the rest is up to God, and He is more than able to finish the job. Developing that strong prayer life takes focus and discipline. No matter where we are with our prayer life—advanced, beginner, or somewhere in between—we can take our conversations with God to a deeper, more peaceful, place.

✒ Consider the situations and people you pray about regularly. Search the Scripture for a specific Bible verse for each one.

✒ What is the hardest part of prayer for you? For some, every aspect seems difficult. Others struggle with certain parts. Earlier in our marriage, my husband and I found it difficult to pray together. But through practice—and not giving up—prayer is now one of the sweetest parts of our marriage. Make a commitment right now to spend time on the parts of prayer that don't come easy. If you have several areas where you struggle, don't try to tackle them all at once. Instead attack them one at a time.

✒ Sometimes our ruffled feathers stem from a lack of control. When we approach prayer expecting to use it as a method of control, we miss the point—and the best part. I would have told you I never used prayer that way, but I would be lying to you and to myself. When I took an honest look at what I was looking to get out of prayer, I found that hidden stumbling block. Prayer is all about releasing, not controlling. Spend some time considering this point and ask God to show you where you need to relinquish control back to Him.

Birds of a Feather—Together
From Rhonda

I have friends who cry cute. They make a little tear in the corner of an eye they can dab away—probably with an embroidered hanky. Me? Ugly crier all the way. I'm talking, red nose, splotches, puffy eyes, and flowing snot. So I got a little tickled at Edie's words, "It wasn't a pretty prayer." Oh how I adore thinking about the fact that my God isn't bugged by my ugly crying—or my ugly prayers. When He sees my ugly tears and that flowing nose, do you know what He does? He hears. What a great truth Edie shares here, that lovely prayers are all about getting the focus off me, and about telescoping it right on Jesus. Beautiful!

Thank You, Father, for hearing every prayer.

Chapter Sixteen

The Unruffliest Identity

Rhonda

Whenever you're feeling under the weather, take it from me: do *not* look up your symptoms on the Internet. Because chances are, you'll find out you've been dead for two days.

I thought I had an average old cold this morning, but I guess not. The Internet tells me something different. It obviously knows about me before I do.

Our information is "out there" these days. Our insides, outsides, past, and present. People's checkered pasts are just a few clicks away from catching up with them. That's why I'm thankful my past isn't all that checkered. I think it's actually more ... well, sort of like a happy plaid. Or a uniquely dyed hounds tooth, maybe. Maybe more paisley. It's the kind of past that's colorful, somewhat interesting, a little confusing—possibly a little dizzying.

A few decades ago, people talked about "finding yourself." I think it was the flower children's way of saying they wanted to do whatever they wanted to do. Nowadays when people talk about finding themselves, they're usually talking about an exhaustive Google search. And I'm guessing it's yet more disturbing when you search and *don't* find yourself. How shocking to study yourself and find out that you're probably not real. At least no one can steal your identity if you don't have one.

Who knew? Well, besides the Internet.

Our real, forever-identity? It can't be stolen. Or lost. Or Google-searched. And as wild as it seems, it can't even die. We are who we are in, through and all because of Jesus. Paul said, "In Him we live and move and have our being' ... 'For we are indeed his offspring'" (Acts 17:28).

No need to do a dizzying search for our identity. We are who we are in Jesus. And in Him, there is, not death, but life! Living, moving, existing as His offspring—His beloved children.

> "See what an incredible quality of love the Father has shown to us, that we should [be permitted to] be named and called and counted the children of God! And so we are!" (1 John 3:1 AMP). I love the paraphrase of that last sentence that shouts it this way: "That's who we really are!" (THE MESSAGE).

Identity crisis? No need to be ruffled by one of those. Who we really are is securely wrapped up, not in who we are at all, but in who Jesus is. Essentially, there are no checkered pasts. No paisley, plaid or polka dot pasts. No hounds tooth. The colorful beauty of the Gospel is that "He made the One who did not know sin to be sin for us, so that we might become the righteousness of God in Him" (2 Corinthians 5:21 HCSB). And, oh glorious thought, we never have to "find ourselves." Our Savior finds us even before we know we need to be found. The work of salvation is all His, covering our off-colored pasts with the blood that makes us clean-white-righteous.

Just a few verses before, Paul reminds us of our "new" past.

> "Therefore, if anyone is in Christ, he is a new creation; old things have passed away, and look, new things have come" (2 Corinthians 5:17 HCSB).

He knows. Not like the Internet "knows." His is a real knowing. He knows us inside-out. The same power that saved us is the power that will influence, change, empower, work, teach, comfort, make new—whatever our need. We can trust Him to save. We can trust Him to know our real needs and meet them.

Oh what security we experience when we rest, unruffled, in Him, and in who He says we are. This is a knowing that guards against ruffles now and ruffles later. Unrufflable!

As for My Sniffles and Me, Me, Me

It's the best kind of unrufflable—even if it doesn't make us "unsniffleable." I looked my cold up on the Internet and now I see it's probably just malaria. Either that or colic.

You might think I'm making this too much about me. Me, my identity, and I.

For the record, I don't think I'm all that vain but I do think the old song is probably about me. I mean really, what if the song actually is about me? A lot of people probably think I'm completely self-absorbed, but I have to tell you, I'm pretty sure I can absorb even more of me. So, not completely absorbed. Not yet.

Whenever I'm struggling with some sort of pride issue, though, I figure a good way to turn things around is to get into a hammock. Just try to hang on to any shred of smugness as you're writhing yourself in or out of a hammock. Nope. Bye-bye, dignity.

It takes some complicated physics to get in that hammock, stay in it, and then get out again. I've never understood physics. That's why my hammock stories so often end with an inelegant face-plant. Yep, bye-bye, dignity and hello, dirt.

Balancing My Identity, My Pride, and That Swing

The challenge for me seems to lie in not totally losing my mind, living somewhere between singing a song I'm sure is about me and eating dirt. Things can so easily get twisted. Yes, the hammock. But also that struggle to wrap our minds around balancing humility and self-abasement, confidence and pride.

Identity. Get back in your rightful place already!

We looked at Romans 12:1-2 in Chapter 6. In verse two, just after Paul has urged us to present our bodies a living sacrifice to God in verse one, he says, "And do not be conformed to this world [any longer with its superficial values and customs], but be transformed and progressively changed [as you mature spiritually] by the renewing of your mind [focusing on godly values and ethical attitudes], so that you may prove [for yourselves] what the will of God is, that which is good and acceptable and perfect [in His plan and purpose for you]" (Romans 12:2 AMP).

So hey, we're not meant to lose our minds. We're meant to renew them. Paul also says, "I tell everyone among you not to think of himself more highly than he should think. Instead, think sensibly," (Romans 12:3 HCSB).

Let's Think This Through

"Think sensibly" is from the Greek, "sophroneo" which means "to save," and "phren" which means "mind." So what we have here is a "saved mind."

Every time we get a bit hung up on tying our identity to self, thinking too often of ourselves, thinking too highly of ourselves, and singing too loudly about ourselves, we can swing it right back around to a sensible place of nonconformity to everything our culture tells us we deserve. We can instead have a saved, transformed, renewed mind—one that understands His will. So this *is* sensible.

We're always the most satisfied in life as we're thinking and operating outside ourselves, less focused on successes vs. face-plants. Life swings in blissful balance as we're instead engaged in the kingdom of Christ and in focusing our every thought on the God who is all.

Andrew Murray said, "Humility is nothing but the disappearance of self in the vision that God is all."

I love Murray's words. I want to climb into that thought and rest peacefully there.

On a Swing and a Prayer

The balance between humility and pride isn't about thinking badly of ourselves or eating dirt. It's certainly not in thinking every song is about me either. We're taught all through scripture to plant our attention in humility securely on the grace of God, to love Him more than anything, to present ourselves wholly to Him, and in all of it, to rely on and fully trust Him for the strength we need.

There's a beautiful visual of that trust in Isaiah 40:31. "But those who trust in the Lord will renew their strength; they will soar on wings like eagles" (HCSB).

We can trust Him to sort out our pride/humility issues too. It's one more little trust-flight on eagle's wings. Or sometimes a flight on hammock swings. Whichever we need. Because He's got this.

Feathering Your Nest

One truth will unruffle any snags in our identity. It's a truth that brings us down a notch when we're too full of ourselves, and it can lift us out of a pit of despair when we're too hard on ourselves and feel we have no value. That truth can be summed up in one word.

His.

This is what your heavenly Father says to you: "Fear not, for I have redeemed you; I have called you by name, you are mine" (Isaiah 43:1).

How many people spend all their energies searching for identity and fighting fruitlessly to balance humility and pride—a right view of self? How many look in a mirror every day with the question, "Who am I, really?" They search for worth and balance in what others think of them, or in a job or status or money or talents. So many search all those people and places, and completely miss the only answer that is true and that truly satisfies: *His.*

The God of the universe says, "you are mine."

Are you letting anything else or anyone else define who you are? Spend some time examining your heart. Can you spot some areas where your beliefs about yourself are based on the world's thinking and worldly philosophies rather than the truth of God?

- Ask the Father who loves and treasures you to correct any wrong thinking about who you are in Christ, and about your true worth. This is a prayer He longs to answer.

- Read the passages of scripture in this chapter again. Will you choose today to believe the truth about yourself?

Birds of a Feather—Together
From Edie

There's no identity crisis about who we are in Christ. And no thief can steal the identity He has given us. The world would have us find ourselves, but we have no reason to go searching. Rhonda helps us remember that God knows where we are and has called us by name. Far from being an issue of self-pride, knowing who I am in Christ if foundational to my faith in Him. No amount of feather ruffling from the world can shake my identity.

Don't ever let me look anywhere but You for my identity and my confidence.

Part Five:
Living Unruffled

A bird's feathers aid it in every aspect of its life, from keeping it warm to providing protection. The most beautiful feathers are generally the strong contour feathers. But their beauty stems mostly from their purpose and their strength.

First, we've mentioned that these feathers shield birds from the damaging effects of the environment—especially the wind. It may seem odd that the part of the bird that makes flight possible also provides much needed protection. Additionally, the gorgeous colors of these feathers provide camouflage and even protection from the harmful rays of the sun.

For us, learning to live unruffled means embracing the function of all our faith feathers. We must care for them—feed our faith. We must allow God to replace them as needed—learn to exercise faith in the new challenges. Even when we're feeling beat down by the world, we can soar.

Chapter Seventeen

Renewed Motivation in Whole-hearted Serving

Rhonda

When I go to an outdoor event in the summer, it's tough for me to get motivated to do anything except sit there and … be hot. I don't suffer pretty. You might say I even suffer ruffly.

Sometimes I try to motivate myself to be the person who guards the food. Shooing flies mostly. Also standing there and being appropriately appalled at how long the mayonnaise has been sitting out.

You'd think the motivation would return as soon as I get back into the gloriously air-conditioned house. But it's not always so. There are comfy chairs in those air-conditioned places that are often the enemies of what I probably need to accomplish.

Sometimes when I'm ready to get up out of a comfy chair and get going on a to-do list, my brain suddenly says, "Whoa, whoa, whoa. Just where do you think you're going?" Then it knocks me back into the chair and brutishly sends me vibes about potato chips, pizza pockets, and mocha latte smoothies. I can hear my brain snickering manically at that point because it knows it always has me at "smoothie."

But hey, just because I'm still sitting doesn't mean I'm not working [insert sound of crunching chips] because at least I'm thinking really hard about all the stuff I need to do [insert sound of smoothie-slurp].

Inside/Outside Motivation

Whenever I get into serious ruffly scuffles with my brain over a to-do list, I know it's time to check my motivation again. Is everything on the to-do list born of His calling? Why do I do what I do? And when I'm serving the Lord and loving on His people, am I really serving Him, or am I trying to impress others? Or am I doing it because it's expected of me? Or so I won't be thought of as unspiritual?

This is the reminder—more to me than to you—that it's not a bad idea to regularly do a good motive analysis. As a matter of fact, it's biblical. "Search me, O God, and know my heart! Try me and know my thoughts! And see if there be any grievous way in me, and lead me in the way everlasting!" (Psalm 139:23-24).

I never want to be careless or complacent or lazy when it comes to enthusiastically climbing out of the chair and serving. It's not because I never get tired. It's because I never fall out of love. When we're working for Him out of love, even when it's difficult, there's great satisfaction. It's one big way to live unruffled even in the busiest or the most trying, ruffling seasons. Whether I'm monitoring mayonnaise or washing feet, I want to do it with everything I've got out of love for my Savior. Not for a pat on the back or an "atta girl" even. But most especially for that moment of worship. Surrender. Obedience. Love.

My Servant-Leader Leader

Jesus is my example. The Creator of the universe dressed Himself as a servant, then washed a bunch of dirty disciple-feet. And then He said, "If I then, your Lord and Teacher, have washed your feet, you also ought to wash one another's feet. For I have given you an example, that you should do just as I have done to you" (John 13:14-15).

My motivation? I can ask for it. It comes from Him—from the inside. Not inside the house, inside me, and by the power of His indwelling presence.

Sometimes I do have to be willing to take on some discomfort. I might have to get out of the chair and take a little heat, as it were, and allow serving Him to be an act of worship and a response of love. "Whatever you do, do it from the heart, as something done for the Lord and not for people" (Colossians 3:23 CSB). We're living out His Gospel from the heart as we follow Jesus all the way to the cross—sometimes via the wash bucket and towels.

That's my goal. Note it right here, friends. I want to serve sweeter. And—when I have to—I hope to suffer prettier. You can make a note of that too.

And a Note About Notes

Speaking of notes, did you ever get one from your child's school and secretly hope it was about anything but a project?

Minor behavior infraction. Please let it be a minor behavioral infraction.

Oh, that four-word note that casts dread deep into the heart of a parent:

SCIENCE NOTEBOOK DUE MONDAY.

Because bye-bye, weekend.

It's funny how we try to convince ourselves that it's *not* going to require more from parent than from child. Denial is interesting that way. When my kids were younger, I would eventually work through the stages and make it to acceptance. Acceptance that it's a weekend of glue—and lots of it. And some researching, some clipping, some labeling and some Extra Strength Tylenol. Maybe also some crying. Not sure whose.

The Science of the Servant-Leader

Those assignments require much of us. But there's a lovely science involved when we observe, experiment, and conclude that in even the smallest life minutiae, as we lead responsibly, we're teaching how to become responsible leaders. It's like the spiritual scientific method—with all beakers on full burner. At the same time, as we serve well, we're demonstrating how to be unruffled selfless servants. That unruffled living can inspire more unruffled living in those around us and under our influence.

How do we lead responsibly? The truth is, I can only lead well as I'm God-led.

How can we model servanthood? It's an undeniable fact that I can only serve well as I'm God-empowered by my Servant-King.

Paul's "schooling" in Philippians 2 has inspired and convicted me regularly since I was a teen (and working on *my* science notebooks). "Do nothing out of selfish ambition or conceit, but in humility consider others as more important than yourselves. Everyone should look out not only for his own interests, but also for the interests of others" (Philippians 2:3-4 CSB).

Everyone should look out not only for his own science notebooks ...

Will This Be on the Test?

I think one of the best tests of how "servant-y" my heart is at any given moment is my willingness to lead--without expecting to be treated as a leader. By not insisting on status or recognition or payback or anything at all in return. By not asking for even a free weekend or an A+. The real question: Am I willing to serve when it's probably going to cost me—even when it's going to cost me deeply and dearly?

Serve? Or ruffle? The next verses in that Philippians 2 passage reveal my assignment—my motivation and my empowerment. It's all in Christ Jesus.

> "Adopt the same attitude as that of Christ Jesus, who, existing in the form of God, did not consider equality with God as something to be exploited. Instead he emptied himself by assuming the form of a servant, taking on the likeness of humanity." (Philippians 2:5-6 CSB).

It was servanthood that took the King all the way to a humiliating cross. And when I "adopt the same attitude," and allow this glorious Servant-King to work it in and out and through me, I can bypass the denial and the crying and any other ruffled and misdirected response. Bye-bye, pride.

No hypothesis about it, in raising our kids, those times pride was in check, weekends were grand—project or no project. You should also know that I'm mostly kidding about the projects I did with my children. Because in the middle of a lot of tears, toil, and Tylenol, we had concentrated time together we might not have had. In essence: Hello, weekend. We explored a sweet handful of topics together. I had five kids, so that does mean my fingers were a tad glued together on a lot of Mondays. That's okay. Especially since on that last science notebook, I got an A. I mean my son. My son got an A.

Feathering Your Nest

How often have you asked yourself the question, "Why do I do what I do?" And the follow-up question, "Is there something I feel God has called me to do—some place He's asked me to lead out—where I'm sitting back and waiting? And then there's the follow-up-follow-up question, "What am I waiting for?"

There is great blessing in answering the Father's call to service. Blessing for the one He calls, and blessing for the people that we will serve.

> "For God is not unjust so as to forget your work and the love which you have shown for His name in ministering to [the needs of] the saints (God's people), as you do. And we desire for each one of you to show the same diligence [all the way through] so as to realize and enjoy the full assurance of hope until the end, so that you will not be [spiritually] sluggish, but [will instead be] imitators of those who through faith [lean on God with absolute trust and confidence in Him and in His power] and by patient endurance [even when suffering] are [now] inheriting the promises" (Hebrews 6:10-12 AMP).

Let's run our motivation, our service, and our leadership through the wringer of this passage in Hebrews 6 a few times. Write out the points of calling. Then list the blessings.

Are there any feet you should be washing? Anytime we need an extra dose of Jesus motivation for that kind of service, we've got it right here in the words of Jesus, "So if I, your Lord and Teacher, have washed your feet, you also ought to wash one another's feet. For I have given you an example, that you also should do just as I have done for you" (John 13:14-15).

The blessing? It's mentioned there, too, in the next couple of verses: "Truly, truly, I say to you, a servant is not greater than his master, nor is a messenger greater than the one who sent him. If you know these things, blessed are you if you do them" (John 13:16-17 CSB).

Ask the Father for His empowering and equipping to "adopt the same attitude" as our Servant-King. This would be a great prayer to write out in a journal. Add the date and later come back to marvel at how the Lord answers.

Birds of a Feather—Together
From Edie

Motivation from the inside out—wisdom we can live with. God doesn't ignore our service for others—even if it sometimes feels like a thankless job. But even more than what we do, God is interested in our heart motivation. Serving from the love we carry for Christ gives us an endless supply of energy. It's only when we work from our strength that we find ourselves ruffled and bedraggled, gasping for strength.

Don't let me misplace my motivation or ever try apart from You.

Chapter *Eighteen*

Waterproof Your Feathers for the Storms of Life

Edie

I love rainy days. The rest of my family are sun worshippers, but I look forward to those cozy days, hemmed with rain and raveled in jagged strips of lightning.

I especially love walking in the rain. There's something comforting in huddling beneath a large umbrella, safe and dry, while the world around me is wet. One of my favorite places to walk is at a nearby nature preserve. There are lots of animals and some beautiful wetlands that support colonies of ducks, geese, and great blue herons.

Heedless of the Rain

I was there one drizzly morning and had the opportunity to notice how completely unconcerned the birds were with the rain. As I watched, the water drops beaded up on their silky smooth feathers and rolled right off. Even without an umbrella, they stayed dry and warm.

A little time on the Internet doing research led me to the reasons rain doesn't soak through a bird's feathers.

First they practice preening. Birds have a special gland that contains an oily substance. They use their beaks and in some instances their talons, to coat their feathers with this protection. It requires a daily application to keep their feathers in order and waterproof.

During the preening process, in addition to coating the feathers with the oil, a bird works the feathers into place, making certain they lie flat and straight. The overlapping quality of unruffled feathers is vital to keeping water out and body heat in.

Of course this process is a perfect picture of what God does with us. Preening is similar to the daily interaction every believer needs with God. When we spend regular time with Him, He soothes our souls, anointing us with the oil of His presence. He smooths our ruffled feathers and helps insulate us from the storms of life. He won't always stop the storms from coming, but He does give us the protection we need to stay unruffled and waterproof. "You prepare a table before me in the presence of my enemies. You anoint my head with oil; my cup overflows" (Psalm 23:5 NIV).

God's Anointing in Stormy Times

I learned how God protects in the storm first hand when my friend and her daughter were taken from us. I remember the day so well. The telephone rang before daybreak, pulling me from a deep sleep. Kim asked if we could meet.

"Sure. When and where?"

"I'm on your front porch right now,"

I threw on a robe, rushed down the stairs, and opened the door.

"What is it? What's happened?" No one shows up on your porch—before dawn—with good news.

"It's Jennifer. She and Abby are missing."

I wanted to sink to the ground right there in the entryway, but made it into the den and perched on the edge of the couch. That was the beginning of a years-long nightmare. Jennifer was our best friend. She, her husband, and their daughter had moved to Colorado the previous year. Now her husband had come home from work the night before and found a gruesome scene with no sign of his wife and daughter.

Jennifer and I had met several years earlier. Her family and mine had joined our church around the same time. We were kindred spirits. We could talk about anything, and she was one of my first prayer partners. She also was an encourager. She would often say, "God called you to write, and He called me to pray for your writing."

The week she disappeared was a nightmare. I wanted desperately to do something, but there really wasn't anything to do except pray. So we rallied the prayer warriors, did everything we could to support her husband long distance since he discouraged us from coming out to Colorado, and scoured the Internet for news. My house became the place to gather, to wait for information. The only constant was prayer. Everyone who came in my front door prayed. Sometimes we prayed in groups, sometimes in pairs. But it was always the same petition. Please God, let us know she's safe.

One afternoon later that week, I took my son to a friend's house to play. He needed to get out, even if I was reluctant to leave. Although the family was new to the church, I had gotten to know the mother pretty well.

Rhonda stood on her front porch when I pulled into her driveway. Her son rushed over to open the van door and the two boys took off around the house. I went up to the porch to work out the details of my son's visit. "Come on in and have a cup of coffee," she said. "I know you're exhausted."

"I can't stay." I looked at my watch. Even though I was glad I'd brought my son, I didn't want to be away from the phone, just in case we got word.

"I understand." She leaned a shoulder against the wall. "I'm so sorry about Jennifer."

I blinked back tears, frustrated that after so much crying they still came so readily. "I know. Just pray."

She gave me a quick hug. "That's what I wanted to talk to you about." I must have looked confused because she smiled and continued. "Prayer, I need to talk to you about prayer."

"Sure," I said, not sure at all where this conversation was headed. "What about prayer?"

Rhonda shifted her weight and folded her arms. "I know this is going to sound weird, but I don't have a choice." She shook her head. "God has called me to pray for you."

"Thank you." I'm ashamed to admit that my answer was automatic. "But I'm fine. It's Jennifer and Abby we need to pray for."

"Oh, I'm praying for them, I promise. But this is different. God was specific. I'm supposed to pray for you." She frowned, as if she was trying to remember a direct quote. "God called you to write, and He called me to pray for your writing."

Those words almost brought me to my knees. I remember grabbing the porch railing for support as those words echoed in my mind. Those words, they were Jennifer's words and yet they weren't. That day I heard the Voice behind the words.

Soon I was back in my minivan and on the way home without noticing how much time passed. I pulled into my driveway, turned off the engine and sat. It was quiet, inside and out. The tears rolled down my cheeks unchecked as I mourned the loss of my best friend. I now knew where Jennifer was. From the moment Rhonda spoke those words, I felt the certainty that Jennifer wouldn't be found alive. God had answered my prayer and how I wished He hadn't. But knowing brought a kind of comfort—after all, I knew she and Abby were safe.

Walking Through the Storms

God won't always stop the storms from coming, but He gives us the protection we need to weather them. Sometimes they're just inconvenient rain showers, at other times they are devastating hurricanes that leave our lives in shambles. With God, size doesn't matter. He's able to protect us no matter what. It was prayer that got me through those stormy days. Spending time in prayer with God and through the prayers of those who knew how badly I hurt.

Feathering Your Nest

In stormy weather or clear—we're sheltered by Him. Once we put our faith in God, that relationship becomes the oil that anoints our hearts and minds. That's not to say bad things don't happen, they definitely do. But we're protected by His peace and the knowledge of His perfect love for every one of us.

Take time right now to do a little preening. Open the Bible and allow His protecting oil to flow onto your ruffled feathers. Let Him lead you beside still waters. Turn over the storms you're facing right now and allow God to provide the insulation you need.

Take a look at your daily schedule. Where does God fit into your routine? Where should He fit in? Commit right now to rearrange your life to make spending time with Him a priority. When you do, your feathers will be ready for the stormy days ahead.

Birds of a Feather—Together
From Rhonda

Let me drive home the point again here, that when sin was introduced into this world in the garden, the curse began. Since then, living in a world that's groaning under the influence of that sin, storms do happen. Even if we've surrendered our hearts and lives to Christ and our personal sin-debt has been gloriously paid, we might get wet. A sin-cursed world will sometimes splash. But we will never, never drown. Because of the cross of Jesus, our destiny is sure. And though the mascara may run and the hair stick to our faces in ugly wet clumps, we can rest unruffled in every storm.

Thank You, Jesus.

Chapter *Nineteen*

Be the Wind Beneath Someone Else's Wings

Rhonda

If it hadn't required law school and … you know … *brains* and whatnot, I would be a lawyer right now. Except I wanted to do it exclusively so I could someday say to a colleague, "See ya later, litigator."

It's all about the line. Even though I would've delivered that line with way too much eyebrow movement. It's probably just as well that I didn't become a lawyer. For many reasons, yes, but on top of all those, some people might've considered it the wrong motivation for a career choice. But come on, the line! Plus, somewhere in the course of that long-term legal education I could've also used the line, "After while, legal file." So—totally worth it.

Could I go ahead and admit how ruffled I can get when it comes to motivating people to serve? What is the secret to stirring people to move? How many times do we offer forever-heaven-points, for instance, to get nursery workers? Or offer to wash people's cars to get them to keep Sunday School records? Or pay for their kids' college so they'll help with the 7th grade boys' sleep-over?

I Can Do It! Wait, No—I Can't

It's easy to get our feathers ruffled when people don't do what we want them to. Especially when we're in a leadership role. I've been

133

there. With the guilting and the bribing and the manipulating—even brilliantly arguing the case. The most brilliantly argued cases still don't work for long when we're seeking to provoke people to serve. Those arguments don't even work for me on *myself.*

Do you ever try to reason with your motivation?

"I'm going to do that project right now! And clean my house! Do every piece of laundry! Paint the kids' bedrooms! Paint the entire church fellowship hall!"

Then before you get to even the first project, your motivation sasses back to you, "Nah, just kidding, bro. What I meant was that I'm gunna get on Facebook for an hour and then take a little siesta."

"RIP, motivation."

Samuel's Closing Arguments

In Samuel's final public speech in 1 Samuel—his "closing arguments"—he encourages his people: "Above all, fear the LORD and worship him faithfully with all your heart; consider the great things he has done for you" (1 Samuel 12:24 CSB).

Anytime we're interested in seeing motivation resurrected—ours or others'—thinking about (considering) our great God and all He's done is the perfect start. Real motivation to work/serve begins with an "all your heart" love for Him. Love for God beats guilt or manipulation any day of the week.

When people serve out of obligation or they feel used or manipulated, not only is the service half-hearted, but it's not likely to continue long. It's exhausting, draining, often fruitless, and can end in burnout.

Serving with Unruffled Gladness

Wholehearted service produces unruffled joy in jobs big and small. Our God notices that kind of work. We read about it in the Hebrews passage we looked at in the "Feathering Your Nest" section of Chapter 17. The Christian Standard Bible puts it this way. "For God is not unjust; he will not forget your work and the love you demonstrated for his name by serving the saints—and by continuing to serve them" (Hebrews 6:10 CSB). He will not forget your work. The service described there is one that grows out of love for the Lord—for *His* name. And it's a service, according to the last part of the verse, that keeps going.

As we make our life all about our infinite, all-knowing, all-loving God who is worthy of our love and praise and service, that love and praise and service happens organically. *He* is our motivation, so serving becomes our joy. "Serve the LORD with gladness and delight; Come before His presence with joyful singing" (Psalm 100:2 AMP).

We can weigh ourselves and others down with guilt and pressure. Or we can get free so that service is part of joy-filled worship. You can't stop a worshipper from loving on those babies in the nursery or hanging out with 7th grade boys. They do it with dedication. Not litigation.

Listen to the Arguments—Can I Get a Hearing?

When it comes to dealing well with people and inspiring others to serve, I often feel convicted. Not exactly in the most legal terms of the word "convicted," but still convicted. My conviction comes in the area of listening.

We don't always think of listening as a way to serve people, or a way to honor God, or as an element of an unruffled life. But without listening to the Father, through His Spirit and through His Word, there are only ruffles. And without listening to people, we end up in a one-sided "preach," rather than building a legit connection where we show love and godly leadership.

So I definitely should not admit to this, but sometimes when someone says the words, "to make a long story short," I figure I'm going to need to cancel my plans for the rest of the day. Does that ever happen to you?

I know what you're thinking. You're thinking I'm not one to talk about long stories or the people who tell them. I'm known for being more than a little on the wordy side. And still, even in a personal conversation, I sometimes have trouble listening to others whose presentations are longer than three minutes. Especially if they don't have visual aids.

People. Give me a cartoon. Flannel board, maybe. A graph or a nice pie chart. Please. Not necessarily because of my short attention span or anything, but it's always good to be—hey, now I want pie.

To Make a Long Story Pie

Speaking of the abrupt segues of people with short attention spans, I opened the microwave the other day and found a piece of pie in there. I know I don't have the best track record when it comes to whatever in the world I've left in the microwave. Shoot. But there I was, wondering, *where in the world did this pie come from?* Then I remembered that I put it in there two days before. Wow, bet that pastry is done now.

All focus deficits aside (again), I really am trying to learn to listen better. Whether or not I get the pie chart. Or the pie. James 1:19 tells me, "Everyone must be quick to hear, slow to speak" (HCSB). And boy oh boy, can I get those backwards.

So how can we be "quick to hear" and "slow to speak"? Listen faster? Speak slower?

Actually, I'm quite sure it's not a matter of speed. More often we need to simply replace the speaking with the listening.

I'm typically putting together some kind of impressive response in my mind while someone is still talking. All too often I should still be listening, and instead I let my words take control of my brain and my lips.

Letting our words take control is letting our flesh take control. And you can bet sin won't be far behind. Words out-of-control lead to being uncaring and unkind. They lead to anger and all kinds of sinful responses on both sides of a conversation. James connects words and the angry responses we need to avoid in that verse when he calls us to be: "quick to hear, slow to speak, and slow to anger," and the next verse explains that "man's anger does not accomplish God's righteousness" (James 1:19, 20 HCSB).

Many Words, Many Ruffles

Proverbs 10:19 says it well. "When there are many words, sin is unavoidable, but the one who controls his lips is wise" (HCSB). If we desire to live well—to "accomplish God's righteousness"— maybe we don't need to be as concerned about an attention deficit as we are about giving our attention in the right direction. We're not walking in righteousness, nor encouraging it in others, when we let our me-focused words run wild, when we focus on having our say rather than finding ways we can use our words to build up another person, and when we let our focus slip away from genuinely caring for the people the Lord has called us to love.

O Lord, may my focus be always on You. Use my words to love others in Your name.

I do want to love others with sweet words of grace, Proverbs 16:24-style. "Gracious words are like a honeycomb, sweetness to the soul and health to the body."

And forgive me if my listening is a tad faulty here, but to me, that sounds a whole lot like pie.

Feathering Your Nest

Romans 13:8-10 in The Message sums up the "law code" well. The sum? Love.

> "Don't run up debts, except for the huge debt of love you owe each other. When you love others, you complete what the law has been after all along. The law code—don't sleep with another person's spouse, don't take someone's life, don't take what isn't yours, don't always be wanting what you don't have, and any other "don't" you can think of— finally adds up to this: Love other people as well as you do yourself. You can't go wrong when you love others. When you add up everything in the law code, the sum total is love" (THE MESSAGE)

Every bit of true and unruffled loving is a result of the Lord and the love He gives us for His people. Worship is the most genuine path to service. Worshipping Him and considering all He has done helps us know Him better. Knowing Him better always causes us to love Him more—and that creates in us a heart that longs to serve Him. It equips us as well to better inspire others to serve.

Set aside a time to worship your Creator today. Think about all He has done. Ask Him to allow you to know Him better and love Him well in service. Pray that He will allow your love for Him to inspire others to serve Him.

How does this kind of worship affect your ability to love and serve those people who rub your feathers the wrong way?

How can becoming a good listener directly affect the way we serve Christ personally? How could it affect the way we inspire others to serve?

Could I also encourage you, if you're in a ruffly season, to not neglect grabbing a friend's hand? We were built to do life together—even the most harried parts. Maybe especially those. We never take a break from loving people. Allowing others to exercise their God-given gifts to show love to us can be a blessing all the way around. You might find it soothing some feathers in the most beautiful and unexpected ways. Is there someone you think the Lord might be calling you to minister to or serve? Is there someone who He has been using to love on and minister to you? Thank Him for all the lovely aspects of this kind of feather-smoothing.

Birds of a Feather—Together
From Edie

Unruffled joy—that's a phrase I'd use to describe Rhonda every time. Her enthusiasm in serving God shines through her life and her writing. As I glean insight—along with her readers—I'm challenged and blessed to live in her unruffled example.

Let each of us practice being an example of unruffled joy!

138

Chapter *Twenty*

Ready to Walk Through the Storms Unruffled

Edie

Nothing can ruffle our feathers like a storm. And some seasons of life bring a series of storms. These events don't have to be hurricane size to be exhausting. Sometimes it's the tiny, ongoing circumstances that sap us the most. Like single drops of water in series have the ability to wear away solid rock, so these recurring events deplete our energy and—in the process—draw our focus away from God.

Doing life apart from God is the true source of ruffled exhaustion. And the tiny disturbances offer the strongest temptation to handle life ourselves. Most of us have learned to take the big stuff to God. But we still hesitate to bother Him with the small.

One of the most intense struggles in my life came while my dad was in the final stages of Alzheimer's. My mother was his primary caregiver, but my sister and I were actively helping support her. I was under contract and finishing a book.

I'd done what I thought was a pretty good job of turning over my stress to God. I was *prayed up* in regard to Daddy's illness, my mother's exhaustion, and my book. The rest of life I was handling on my own. Only I wasn't. It seemed the smallest issue would set my feathers flying in all different directions as I pecked at the people who were trying to help.

After one particularly trying morning at the assisted living facility, my family urged me to take a break and go get lunch—

alone. At the time I thought they were giving me space. Looking back I realize they were probably trying to get a break from me.

I hopped into my car and almost immediately the irritations seemed to mount. I was almost out of gas, there was a line at the gas station, the pump was out of receipt paper. Traffic was bad, drivers were rude, and the drive-through line at my favorite fast food restaurant wrapped around the building. I didn't care. I wanted chicken and chicken I was determined to have—even if I had to wait an hour.

Parking and going inside would have solved the long line problem, but I was a mess and I knew it. I didn't want to show up in a public place with rumpled clothes and rumpled feathers. I wanted something in life to be easy, but it didn't seem that was going to happen.

The drive through line eventually divided into two lanes and of course I chose the lane that never seemed to move. For some reason, that was the straw that broke the camel's back. Sitting in my car, I lost it. I cried. I ranted. I'm ashamed to say I think I even raised my fist at God. I accused Him of picking on me, of forgetting me—the impossibility of someone picking on me while simultaneously ignoring me wasn't something I considered in that middle of feather-flying fit.

As my sobs turned to hiccups, I felt the voice of God whispering into my soul. He reminded me that I'd been trying to handle all the details of my crazy life on my own—apart from Him. He gently stroked my feathers and reminded me He cared about all of my life, not just the big stuff. I felt peace beginning to return, but I asked Him for some confirmation. I wanted something odd, but obviously from Him, that told me He did care about all the unimportant—exhausting—parts of my crazy life.

I pulled to the window to pay and pick up my order and the clerk gave me a tentative smile. I cringed because I realized a lot of people must have noticed the woman in the car having a melt-down. "The lady in front of you paid for your order. But she was adamant I give you this message. She wanted you to know that whatever you're going through right now, God knows, and He cares."

Somehow I managed to thank her through my tears and drove off. I parked at the edge of the lot because I was crying so hard I couldn't see to drive. But it was worth the kerfuffle. God had reminded me—in a way I'll never forget—that He cares about everything—tiny and big—that is happening in my life.

Peace never comes to us apart from God

If I am not in close communion with God, then nothing goes smoothly. When I flutter away, feathers ruffled by emotions and circumstances, I know that I have drifted from the one who makes life smooth. I've wandered away from my anchor, my foundation, my Jesus.

"Peace I leave with you; My peace I give to you; not as the world gives, do I give to you. Let not your heart be troubled, nor let it be fearful" (John 14:27).

Peace is an on-going process

Finding rest in God's peace it is not a permanent condition. Just as my circumstances constantly change, so does my quest for peace and the steps I take to renew it. But my ability to live in it depends on me, never on God's whim.

> "Now may the God of peace Himself sanctify you entirely; and may your spirit and soul and body be preserved complete, without blame at the coming of our Lord Jesus Christ. Faithful is He who calls you, and He also will bring it to pass" (1 Thessalonians 5:23-24).

Peace is attainable

God is faithful and able to do what He promises. He promises us peace in every circumstance and I am living proof that He is able.

How do we really know it's attainable? This is the verse I go to when I need to remember that God and God alone is my sustainer. "I love Thee, O Lord, my strength. The Lord is my rock and my fortress and my deliverer, my God, my rock, in whom I take refuge;

141

my shield and the horn of my salvation, my stronghold. I call upon the Lord, who is worthy to be praised, and I am saved from my enemies" (Psalm 18:1-3).

Here's what this verse says to me:

- First He is described as my strength. He is the *power* in my life, without Him I am weak.

- Next God is described as my rock. He is my *foundation*. With Him at the core of my life, my feathers will never be in disarray.

- God is described as my fortress. He is the *safe place* in which I can hide. I don't have to run to Him with the big things. I can seek the safety of His presence at the slightest whisper of wind,

- He is my deliverer. In all ways and in all instances, He is my *Savior*. Of course He has provided eternal salvation and that is a gift beyond price. But His deliverance doesn't stop there. He delivers me from my distress.

- The psalm goes on to say He is my shield. He is my *defender*. He stands between me and the ill-winds that blow my way.

- He is the horn of my salvation. He is the *announcer* of my salvation.

- He is my stronghold. He is my *support*.

Life is made up of going and doing. Busyness is part of life, but living unruffled in the midst of that busyness was always God's plan. Busyness and chaos are never the opposite of peace. When we are anchored in Christ, peace isn't external, it flows from an endless well and affects every person and every situation we encounter.

Living unruffled ultimately is not about me. It's about Christ in me, flowing through me, and bringing His peace to the world.

Feathering Your Nest

Turning over the big stuff to God is often simpler than bothering Him with life's little irritants. But when we begin to pick and choose which part of life we yield to God, we always get into trouble.

- As you look at the way you've been doing life, answer these two questions honestly. Do you give everything to God to handle? If not, why?

- Examine the parts of life you realize you have *not* given to God and take time right now to lay them at His feet.

- Think of a time when you or someone else walked into a difficult situation and instead of adding to the chaos, brought peace. Study the circumstances and everything you remember about that time. Then ask God to help you do the same when you're faced with feather-ruffling situations.

Birds of a Feather—Together
From Rhonda

From the drippety-drip-drip of a feather-rustling storm, to winner-winner, chicken dinner! Only God.

That, reader-friends, is the message of this book and the conversations herein, all wrapped up in two words: Only. God. There is no unruffling without a reliance on our Creator. And in Him, even through the kerfuffles, there can be great joy instead of ruffling.

Edie and I would love to continue this conversation with you. We welcome you to connect with us on Facebook, Twitter or any of the other social spots.

Meanwhile, let's snuggle up in the loving arms of our heavenly Father, and—in His presence, by His grace, through His power— live *Unruffled*.

Mighty God. Only You.

Acknowledgments

Edie's Unruffled Acknowledgments

Kirk Melson. I couldn't do life without you. You are truly the wind beneath my wings. You're my joy and the love of my life. Thank you for supporting me, encouraging me, and sometimes pushing me to follow God's path!

Thank you to my amazing kids, Jimmy, Katie, Kirk, Weslyn, and John. You all sure know how to support and encourage! Your love and cheerleading means the world to me.

Thank you to my sister—who's been encouraging and bragging on me since we were kids. I truly don't deserve a sister like you.

Thank you to my mom—one half of the loving duo of creative parents who brought me into this world. You're always a source of inspiration and support.

No book sees the light of day without an amazing team. Bold Vision Books ALWAYS knocks it out of the park. Thank Karen Porter and George Porter—for believing in me, giving me a platform and providing such a great finished book! Also a big shout-out to Amber Weigand-Buckley for the cover design. You took our idea and gave it wings. Thank you! Finally, no author has a better agent than me. David Van Diest, you are the best—giving support, encouragement and wise counsel whenever I ask.

And I'm so grateful to my co-author, Rhonda Rhea. You have been patient, encouraging and oh so wise as we pulled this book together. Every moment writing this book with you was a blessing—life was chaotic and definitely ruffled at times—but the process with you was more unruffled than I could have ever hoped or imagined.

As a writer, I am who I am in a big part because of the community of writers I get to hang with—my AWSA sisters, The Light Brigade women of faith, and my local critique group. There truly are too many of you to thank individually. You all are my heart.

A big thank you also goes to my prayer team and those at Simpsonville First Baptist. You all believed in me long before I believed in myself. You are all such a sweet, sweet blessing.

As always, the best for last. Thank you to my amazing Savior and Lord, Jesus Christ. He called me, equipped me and if there is ever anything good that comes through the words I pen, it's from Him. I'm amazed at the invitation to join You at work and marvel that You can use one such as me.

Rhonda's Unruffled Acknowledgments

Richie Rhea. My hero. How would life and ministry look without this person partnering with me? I shudder to think. Oh the love, encouragement, and support of this remarkably wonderful, godly man! I am so, so blessed. And so, so grateful.

Big thank yous to the rest of my amazingly supportive fam. Andy, Amber, Asa and Amos Rhea, Jordan and Camille Clark Rhea, writer-bud, Kaley Rhea, Allie, Derek, Emerson and Oswyn McMullin, Daniel, Olivia, and Ainsley Rhea—these peeps are all the best pray-ers/supporters/encouragers on the planet.

I appreciate Edie and her sweet heart for Jesus so much--what a great co-author. She helped make the writing of this book a sweet joy.

Heartfelt nods of gratitude to the marvelous, unrufflable team at the Bold Vision Books publishing house—especially to Karen Porter and George Porter. Such talent and such heart! Special thanks to Karen Porter for the beautifully significant input that truly made this a better book. Thank yous to Bold Vision, as well, for nabbing the gifted Amber Weigand-Buckley at Barefaced Creative Design for the stunning cover art. And to Amber: Oh my word, stunning indeed—thank you!

As always, I'm thankful for my agent and friend, Pamela Harty, and all those at the Knight Agency who help make it possible for me to do what I love to do.

Thank you, AWSA, the Advanced Writers and Speakers Association, my heart-sisters who share support, knowledge, godly insights and powerful prayers.

More thanks to my church family at Troy First Baptist Church for consistent prayers and encouragement. I don't know what I would do without this sweet church family.

My amazing prayer team—wonderful warrior women! My sincere gratitude to these women for bathing this project in prayer: Janet Bridgeforth, Tina Byus, Diane Campbell, Mary Clark, Theresa Easterday, Chris Hendrickson, Melinda Massey and Peanuts Rudolph.

My deepest gratitude always and ever goes to the One who miraculously redeemed me by His amazing grace, and who empowers the loveliest flight of faith. To my Lord and Savior, Jesus Christ,

Thank You for Your grace, Your incomparable and indescribable peace, and Your constant presence. You are The Unruffler of my soul.

Meet the Authors

Edie Melson is a woman of faith with ink-stained fingers observing life through the lens of her camera. No matter whether she's talking to writers, entrepreneurs, or readers, her first advice is always "Find your voice, live your story." As an author, blogger, and speaker she's encouraged and challenged audiences across the country and around the world. Her numerous books reflect her passion to help others develop the strength of their God-given gifts and apply them to their lives.

She's a leading professional within the publishing industry and travels to numerous conferences as a popular keynote, writing instructor and mentor. Her blog for writers, The Write Conversation, reaches thousands each month and is a *Writer's Digest* Best 101 Websites for Writers. She's a board member of the Advanced Writers and Speakers Association, the Social Media Director for *Southern Writers Magazine*, as well as a the director of the Blue Ridge Mountains Christian Writers Conference. She and husband Kirk have been married 36+ years and raised three sons. They live in the foothills of the Blue Ridge Mountains in SC where they love to hike and wander the mountains. Connect with her on her website, www.EdieMelson.com and through social media.

Rhonda Rhea is an award-winning humor columnist for great magazines such as *HomeLife, Leading Hearts, The Pathway,* and many more. She is the author of 16 other books, including the new romantic comedy *Off-Script & Over-Caffeinate*d and the award-winning *Turtles in the Road*—both co-authored with her daughter, Kaley Rhea. Rhonda and Kaley have also teamed up with Bridges TV host, Monica Schmelter, for the *Messy to Meaningful* books (with a new one coming soon). Rhonda also co-authors the *Fix Her Uppe*r series with Beth Duewel. They are looking forward to next season's *A Fix Her Upper Christmas*.

In addition to regular TV appearances, Rhonda speaks at conferences and events from coast to coast, serves on many boards and committees, and works as well as a publishing consultant. She lives near St. Louis with her pastor/husband, has five grown children, and says she's working toward a bumper crop of grandbabies.